The Runner's Cookbook
Winning Recipes from Some of the World's Best Athletes

Compiled and Edited by Alison Wade

Published by www.lulu.com.

Any corrections to this publication will be available at www.runnerscookbook.com.

All photos by Alison Wade and Parker Morse. Photos on pages 3, 13, 14, 16, 19, 30, 31, 32, 48, 59, 64, 82, 86, 94, and 96 used with permission of New York Road Runners.

ISBN: 978-1-4357-1640-7

In Memory of Ryan Shay

In addition to being a hero and friend to many, Ryan Shay was a champion on the roads and track. He won the 2001 NCAA 10,000m title and was a nine-time All-American for the University of Notre Dame. During his professional running career, Shay won the 2003 USA Marathon Championship, the 2003 and 2004 USA Half Marathon Championships, the 2004 USA 20k Championship, and the 2005 USA 15k Championship.

On November 3, 2007, five-and-a-half miles into the 2008 U.S. Olympic Team Trials — Men's Marathon in New York City, Shay collapsed and died suddenly, due to a heart condition. It was an event that shocked and deeply saddened the entire running community.

Half of the proceeds from this cookbook will go to the Ryan Shay Memorial Fund, to help Shay's family undertake special projects in his memory.

In Support of Jenny Crain

Jenny Crain, a popular member of the professional running community, suffered serious head and neck injuries after being hit by a car while training in Milwaukee, Wisconsin on August 21, 2007.

Crain is a four-time U.S. Olympic Trials qualifier in the marathon and a two-time qualifier on the track. She represented the U.S. in the marathon at the 2005 World Track & Field Championships, and was the top U.S. finisher at the 2004 ING New York City Marathon. Crain finished 11th at the 2004 U.S. Olympic Marathon Trials in a personal record of 2:37:36.

As of this writing, Crain has made great strides in her recovery, but still has a long way to go. Half of the proceeds from this cookbook will go to the Jenny Crain "Make It Happen" Fund, to help Crain and her family with her continued care, treatment, and recovery.

Contents

Contents

Contents

Main Dishes, continued

Contents

Main Dishes, continued

Side Dishes, Appetizers, Beverages, and Snacks

Desserts

Contents

Desserts, continued

Breakfast, Breads, & Muffins

Banana Chocolate Chip Muffins — Jenny Crain

INGREDIENTS

1-1/2 c. mashed ripe banana (about 3-1/2 bananas)

2/3 c. packed light brown sugar

1/3 c. unsalted butter, melted

1 large egg

1 tsp. vanilla

2 c. flour

2 tsp. baking powder

1 tsp. baking soda

1 tsp. cinnamon

1 tsp. salt

1/2 package of semisweet chocolate chips

Preheat oven to 400°; coat 12-muffin-cup pan with nonstick spray.

Mix together the banana, brown sugar, butter, egg, and vanilla. Sift together the flour, baking powder, baking soda, cinnamon, and salt before adding it to the banana mixture. Mix well and then fold in the chocolate chips.

Bake approximately 20 minutes, until the muffin tops are golden brown.

This is adapted from a recipe which originally appeared in *Muffins A to Z* by Marie Simmons

Jenny Crain holds PRs of 2:37:36 (marathon) and 32:30 (10,000 meters). She has represented the U.S. internationally, was the top U.S. finisher at the 2004 ING New York City Marathon, and is a four-time U.S. Olympic Marathon Trials qualifier.

NOTES ON THIS RECIPE: This recipe was submitted by Cheryl Neumann on Jenny Crain's behalf. Neumann says, "Whenever Jenny and I planned to get together, I would make these muffins. Jenny would take a doggy bag home!"

Pumpkin Chocolate Chip Muffins or Bread — Michelle Sikes

INGREDIENTS

2 c. sugar

2 c. canned pumpkin

1/2 c. canola oil

1/2 c. fat-free vanilla pudding

4 large egg whites

3 c. all-purpose flour

2 tsp. ground cinnamon

1-1/4 tsp. salt

1 tsp. baking soda

1 c. semisweet chocolate chips

Cooking spray

Preheat oven to 350°. Combine the sugar, pumpkin, oil, pudding, and egg whites in a bowl and stir well with a whisk. Lightly spoon flour into dry measuring cups; level with a knife. Combine flour, cinnamon, salt, and baking soda in a medium bowl. Stir thoroughly with a whisk.

Add flour mixture to pumpkin mixture, stirring just until moist. Mix in the chocolate chips.

Spoon batter into two 8x4-inch loaf pans coated with cooking spray. Bake at 350° for 75 minutes or until a wooden pick inserted in the center comes out clean. Cool 10 minutes in pans on a wire rack, and remove from pans. Cool completely on a wire rack. Makes 32 servings.

Michelle Sikes won the 5,000m at the 2007 NCAA Outdoor Track & Field Championships for Wake Forest University. Later that summer, she finished third in the 5,000 at the USA Outdoor Track & Field Championships in a PR of 15:09.29, which qualified her to represent the U.S. at the World Track & Field Championships. Sikes was named a Rhodes Scholar following graduation.

NOTES FROM THE CHEF: This is a favorite of the Wake Forest women's cross country team. Technically it's a recipe for bread, but I usually put the batter in muffin tins instead. I kind of guess about the baking time, but it hasn't turned out disastrously yet!

Blueberry Muffins

Sam Burley

I N G R E D I E N T S

- 1/2 c. soft margarine
- 1-1/4 c. sugar
- 1/4 c. milk
- 1/2 tsp. salt
- 2 eggs
- 2 c. sifted flour
- 2 tsp. baking powder
- 2 c. blueberries

Preheat oven to 350°. Beat eggs, add sugar, milk, and margarine. In a separate bowl, mix flour, salt, and baking powder.

Add first mixture to dry ingredients. Add blueberries.

Bake for approximately 25-30 minutes. Makes 12 muffins.

NOTES FROM THE CHEF: I love these muffins. My mother-in-law makes them with hand-picked frozen blueberries every time I visit.

Sam Burley won the 800 meter title at the 2003 NCAA Outdoor Track & Field Championships for the University of Pennsylvania, and was a five-time All-American. He represented the U.S. at the 2003 World Outdoor Track & Field Championships.

Runner's Scones   Ann Gaffigan

I N G R E D I E N T S

1/2 c. peanut butter

1 c. brown sugar

1 tsp. vanilla

2 scoops protein powder

1 egg

1/4 c. milk

1/8 c. water

2 tbsp. honey

1/2 tsp. baking soda

1 tsp. salt

1 c. wheat flour

3 c. plain oats

2 heaping tbsp. flax seed

1 c. dried fruit—raisins, dried blueberries, dried cranberries, or chocolate chips

Preheat oven to 350°. Mix the peanut butter, brown sugar, vanilla, protein powder, egg, milk, and water until very creamy.

Mix in the honey, baking soda, salt, flour, oats, flax seed, and dried fruit or chocolate chips.

Drop in large spoonfuls onto greased cookie sheets. Bake 10-12 minutes.

Ann Gaffigan, a University of Nebraska graduate, is the 2004 USA champion in the 3,000m steeplechase. She set a then-American record of 9:39.35 in winning that race.

Zucchini Bread

Kristen Nicolini Lehmkuhle

I N G R E D I E N T S

3 eggs

1/2 c. cooking oil

1/2 c. applesauce

3 tsp. vanilla

2 c. grated zucchini

2 c. sugar

3 c. sifted flour

1 tsp. salt

1 tsp. baking soda

3 tsp. cinnamon

2 tsp. nutmeg

1 c. chopped nuts (optional)

Preheat oven to 350°. In one bowl, mix the eggs, cooking oil, applesauce, vanilla, zucchini, and sugar. Let it set until the sugar has partly dissolved (about 15 minutes).

In another bowl, combine the flour, salt, baking soda, cinnamon, nutmeg, and nuts.

Sift the dry ingredients slowly into the wet ingredients. Mix well. Bake for approximately one hour. Makes two loaves.

NOTES FROM THE CHEF: This is my grandmother's recipe. Growing up, my whole family looked forward to my grandparents visiting, and one of the reasons was that my grandmother would bring loaves of her famous zucchini bread. Now I like to make it for Jason and myself to have, especially after a Saturday long run.

Kristen Nicolini Lehmkuhle was a member of Villanova's cross country team which won the 1998 NCAA Cross Country Championship. She was a three-time high school national champion, and more recently finished fifth at the 2008 USA Half Marathon Championship. She is married to Jason Lehmkuhle, who finished fifth at the 2008 U.S. Olympic Marathon Trials.

Date Nut Bread
                                                               Kate O'Neill

I N G R E D I E N T S

1 c. hot coffee

1 c. (or more) of chopped dates

1 tsp baking soda

1 c. sugar

1 tbsp. butter

1 egg

1 tsp. vanilla

1-1/2 c. flour

1 c. chopped walnuts

Preheat oven to 325°. Mix hot coffee, dates, and baking soda. Let this soak while preparing rest of bread (but do not let it soak for more than 10 minutes).

In separate bowl, mix the remaining ingredients. Fold in coffee/date mixture. Pour into loaf pan and bake for 45-60 minutes, or until toothpick comes out clean.

NOTES FROM THE CHEF: This recipe comes from my aunt's husband's mother, Bette Howard. People are always surprised when they see that the recipe is actually fairly healthy. It tastes very moist and rich—it makes a great dessert. The walnuts and coffee make up for the lack of butter.

Kate O'Neill graduated from Yale in 2003 and represented the U.S. in the 10,000 meters at the 2004 Olympic Games. She has run 10,000m in 31:34.37.

Pumpkin Bread/Muffins   Blake Russell

INGREDIENTS

3 c. granulated white sugar

1 c. vegetable oil

4 eggs (or 1 c. egg beaters)

1 lb. canned pumpkin

3-1/2 c. all-purpose flour

1 tsp. baking powder

2 tsp. baking soda

2 tsp. salt

1/2 tsp. ground cloves

1 tsp. ground cinnamon

1 tsp. ground nutmeg

1 tsp. ground Allspice

2/3 c. water

Preheat oven to 350°. In a large bowl, mix the sugar, vegetable oil, eggs, and pumpkin. Once mixed, add the flour, baking powder, baking soda, salt, and spices. Once blended, slowly add the water to the mixture.

Grease pans and pour mixture into two or three nine-inch pans or two muffin pans. Bake loaves for 30-40 minutes, and test with toothpick to determine readiness. Bake muffins for about 15 minutes, until tops are golden brown.

> NOTES FROM THE CHEF: This is one of my favorites for breakfast or snacks. It's really good with some cream cheese frosting for dessert, and it also freezes really well.

Blake Russell finished a heartbreaking fourth at the 2004 U.S. Olympic Marathon Trials, before taking third at the 2008 U.S. Olympic Marathon Trials and qualifying for the U.S. Olympic Team.

"The Webb"

Alan Webb

I N G R E D I E N T S

2 slices whole grain bread

4-6 tbsp. peanut butter

2-3 tbsp. applesauce

Toast both slices of bread. Spread two to three tablespoons of peanut butter on each piece of bread. Then spread one heaping tablespoon of applesauce on each piece, on top of the peanut butter. Chunky or smooth peanut butter works.

The trick is to try to spread on the peanut butter and applesauce fairly quickly after toasting, and then serve while the bread is still warm. Since most of the time the applesauce is refrigerated (unless you just got it from the store and it's at room temperature) when you eat it, you get warm toast and cool apple sauce.

NOTES FROM THE CHEF: This is one of my favorite breakfasts. My dad used to make this for me on weekends when I was a kid.

Alan Webb broke Steve Scott's 25-year-old American record in the mile in 2007 by running 3:46.91. He also holds the U.S. high school mile record of 3:53.43, which he set in 2001.

French Toast

Dick Beardsley

I N G R E D I E N T S

2 eggs

1/2 c. milk

1 tbsp. cinnamon

2 tbsp. vanilla

Sliced wheat bread

Heat skillet, and lightly grease it so the bread doesn't stick. Whisk all ingredients together and dip the bread into the mixture before putting it into the skillet. Cook two or so minutes on each side, until both sides are golden brown.

Sprinkle with powdered sugar and add butter and maple syrup, if desired.

Best known for his 1982 Boston Marathon "Duel in the Sun" with Alberto Salazar (in which he finished second by two seconds), Beardsley is also a London Marathon champion and a two-time Grandma's Marathon champion. His 2:08:53 marathon PR makes him one of the fastest U.S. marathoners of all time.

I N G R E D I E N T S

2 c. all-purpose flour

2 tsp. baking powder

1 tsp. baking soda

1/2 tsp. salt

2-3 tbsp. sugar

2 large eggs

2-3 c. buttermilk—depending on preferred thickness

4 tbsp. unsalted butter or vegetable oil

1-2 c. wild blueberries or other fruit of your choice—optional

Fifteen to 20 minutes before starting to cook, blend the flour, baking powder, baking soda, sugar, and salt in a large bowl.

In a separate bowl, blend the eggs, buttermilk, and the butter or vegetable oil.

Combine the wet and dry ingredients and stir only until well blended. Batter should still have small to medium lumps.

Allow batter to set for 10-15 minutes. This will enable the soda and baking powder to aerate the batter, thus making a lighter Jack Flap.

Heat a well-oiled iron skillet (wipe off excess oil), a Teflon griddle, or heat an electric griddle to 375°. Check griddle heat with a few drops of water, which should sizzle and evaporate almost instantly when the griddle is ready.

Blend in the blueberries or other fruit (raspberries, banana slices, etc.) or just go pure and naked if you don't have/want fruit.

Pour about four ounces of batter for each Jack Flap, keeping enough distance between them so they remain separate. When the pancakes have breaking bubbles on top and are slightly drying at their edge (about two minutes), flip and continue cooking for about another minute or until golden on bottom. (It's okay to check the bottom of the Jack Flap by lifting the edge with a spatula—you don't want to overcook them.)

Repeat with remaining batter, keeping finished pancakes on a covered heatproof plate in oven.

While Flaps are cooking, or beforehand, open one or two eggs into a small bowl—one bowl for each diner who wishes this option.

When the Jack Flaps are all cooked, add an extra teaspoon of oil or butter to griddle and pour eggs on to it, keeping each serving of one or two eggs separate from the others. Cover and let cook only until whites are cooked through—yolk should still be very soft and runny.

Place warm Flaps from oven onto warmed plates. Place eggs on top of stack of Flaps and serve with warm 100% Vermont maple syrup.

One final option is to include a high quality breakfast meat for a nice balance to the sweet syrup. Fresh squeezed orange juice and a robust cup of coffee are the final complement to this amazing breakfast.

Jack Fultz is the winner of the 1976 Boston Marathon, also known as "The Run for the Hoses." The official temperature that day was 91 degrees.

THE STORY BEHIND THE PANCAKES:

I grew up eating a lot of buttermilk pancakes. They were a staple for my family and with seven kids, a large bowl of pancake batter with sides of sausage and potatoes would provide nearly a full meal for all of us.

Naturally I thought my dad's scratch recipe was a well-guarded family secret, handed down over generations, and that only our family enjoyed such sumptuous "griddle cakes," as dad affectionately called them.

As I grew into a competitive runner, I continued to enjoy my buttermilk pancakes. After winning the Boston Marathon in 1976, I considered going commercial with my own "secret recipe." I'd call them Jack's Flaps, credit them for providing me with that extra load of carbs on marathon day, and sell them in specialty shops across the country.

Much to my dismay, I discovered that my "secret recipe" was as common as a pair of size nine Nike running shoes. Look at any cookbook or online recipe for scratch pancakes, and you'll see that they're all pretty much the same. So, with that as a disclaimer against plagarism, I'll also borrow a well-known movie line that applies to my Jack's Flaps' distinct flavor and unique taste—"The secret's in the sauce!"

Just before pouring the batter onto the griddle, slowly mix a few handfuls of wild blueberries into the batter. Then when serving, top with one or two sunny-side up eggs and drown the stack in warmed 100% pure Vermont maple syrup. Oh, makes my toes curl just thinking about 'em.

And should you try these as a pre-race breakfast, be sure to give yourself ample time to digest. The challenge of not stuffing yourself with these delicious morsels might be greater than the challenge of the race you're about to run.

Oatmeal Pancakes

Dathan Ritzenhein

I N G R E D I E N T S

1/2 c. uncooked oats

1/2 c. buttermilk

1/2-3/4 c. milk

1 egg

1 tbsp. oil

2 tbsp. brown sugar

1/2 tsp. salt

1 tsp. baking powder

1 c. flour

1 glob of peanut butter

Combine oats, buttermilk, and milk. Set aside for 15 minutes to soften. Add egg and oil into oatmeal mixture and beat well. Add sugar and salt, then the baking powder and flour. Stir. Then add glob of peanut butter and mix well. Cook in a skillet and enjoy!

Dathan Ritzenhein is a 2004 and 2008 U.S. Olympian and a high school, NCAA, and senior national champion.

Porridge

Jelena Prokopcuka

I N G R E D I E N T S

Oats—as many as you can eat at one time

Nuts—I like walnuts, but you can choose any one

5 pieces dried apricot (naturally dried—they must be brown in color)

1/2 banana

1 tsp. honey

1 tbsp. olive oil or butter

Salt

Put chopped nuts, apricots, sliced banana, and oats into a microwavable glass bowl and mix. Pour in some water—enough that the level of water is just above all of the ingredients. Put the bowl into the microwave for approximately three minutes. Next, add the olive oil and honey and mix. The porridge is ready. Bon appétit!

NOTES FROM THE CHEF: I have never liked porridge, but when I tasted [husband Aleksandr Prokopcuk's] porridge, I understood how good porridge can taste. I think this is the best meal after training.

Jelena Prokopcuka is the 2005 and 2006 ING New York City Marathon champion and a Latvian Olympian.

Soups
&
Salads

Cheese and Vegetable Chowder

Joan Benoit Samuelson

I N G R E D I E N T S

1 c. sliced carrots

1/2 c. butter or olive oil

2 c. chopped cabbage (green)

1 c. sliced onion

1 c. chopped celery

1 c. frozen or fresh peas

1 can creamed corn

2-1/2 c. milk

1 tsp. salt

Dash of pepper

1/4 tsp. thyme

10 oz. cheddar cheese, shredded

Joan Benoit Samuelson won the gold medal in the inaugural women's Olympic Marathon in Los Angeles in 1984.

Sauté carrots in olive oil or melted butter for approximately five minutes. Add the rest of the vegetables and sauté for eight to 10 minutes. Add corn, milk, and seasonings. Heat at low temperature, stir often. Add cheese, stir until melted.

NOTES FROM THE CHEF: This is a favorite family recipe of ours. It was given to me by a Bowdoin friend and track teammate, Ann Gallagher. This cheese and vegetable chowder is delicious, hearty, and easy.

Corn Chowder

Bob Kempainen

I N G R E D I E N T S

1/2 lb. bacon

6-8 medium-sized potatoes, cut into half-inch cubes

1 medium onion, diced

6-8 large carrots, peeled and thinly sliced

2 vegetable bouillon cubes

16 oz. frozen corn

10-12 oz. evaporated milk

NOTES FROM THE CHEF: A friend gave me this recipe when I was just out of school and looking for something cheap, simple, and filling.

Fry bacon and keep the grease. Sequentially brown carrots, onions, and chunks of potatoes in greased frying pan, adding bacon grease as needed. Dump browned vegetables into large cooking pot as you go. Add just enough water to pot to cover vegetables, then gently boil/simmer until potatoes and carrots are cooked. Carrots usually take longer than the potatoes, so brown them longer, or start simmering in pot earlier. Add bouillon cubes.

When vegetables are almost cooked through, add frozen corn and keep simmering until all vegetables are done, more or less. Add the evaporated milk and heat through. Salt and pepper to taste. I probably use a few teaspoons of salt and a couple teaspoons of pepper throughout. Break the bacon into pieces, spread them over each bowl, and serve. I get about six to eight good-sized bowls out of this recipe.

Bob Kempainen is a 2:08:47 marathoner and 1992 and 1996 U.S. Olympian. He won the 1996 U.S. Olympic Marathon Trials.

Friday Night Hawkers Veggie Soup   Victoria Mitchell

I N G R E D I E N T S

20g butter (approximately 1 dessert spoon)

1 onion finely chopped

2 cloves garlic or 2 tsp. crushed garlic

1 potato, peeled and diced

1 small swede (rutabaga), peeled and diced

1 large or 2 small carrots, sliced

1 zucchini, sliced

100g fresh beans or 1 can, drained

4 chicken stock cubes or 4 tsp. of chicken stock powder

400g/14 oz. can of diced tomatoes

4 c. water

Brown onion and garlic. In pot, combine onion, garlic, potato, carrot, and swede (rutabaga). Cook and stir for four to five minutes. Add the zucchini, beans, chicken stock, and water.

Bring to a boil, then reduce heat and simmer for 35-40 minutes, stirring occasionally. Season with salt and pepper to taste.

NOTES FROM THE CHEF:
This soup is probably my favorite, and it's a great way to get all your vitamins and minerals. "Hawkers" refers to the Australian Rules Football League team Hawthorn. My brother, who gave me this recipe, is an avid supporter.

Victoria Mitchell is an Australian steeplechase champion, and she also won the 2005 NCAA steeplechase title for Butler University. She has run 9:30.84 for the 3,000m steeplechase, and has represented Australia at the Commonwealth Games and World Championships.

Great Florida Gator Garbanzo Bean Soup   Keith Brantly

I N G R E D I E N T S

2 qt. vegetable or chicken (preferably University of South Carolina Gamecock) stock

1 qt. of fresh, clean water (optional: swamp water)

5 medium white potatoes, cut into tablespoon-sized cubes

4 15 oz. cans of garbanzo beans, drained

1 large onion, chopped

2 chorizo sausages (preferably made with Arkansas Razorback meat), thinly sliced*

10 strands of saffron

*Sausage is optional for the vegetarians, but you don't know what you're missing! Marinated Georgia Bulldog meat is a worthy substitute.

Combine all of the ingredients in a large pot. Heat until boiling, then cover tightly, sing the University of Florida fight song, reduce to simmer for 45 minutes or until the potatoes are done...or until you can't stand waiting because the smell is so darn good.

Season to taste, but make it fun. Experiment with your favorite seasonings. Start with Season-All. Salt will be your friend; watch the blood pressure though.

Enjoy with bread and a huge glass of red wine. Keep a couch and pillow close by as this recipe will make you pass out and dream of football and basketball national championship victories and running the marathon in the Olympics...Oh, I'm sorry...I forgot...Those aren't dreams anymore!

> Keith Brantly is a 2:12:31 marathoner and 1996 Olympian. He has won USA titles in the 10,000, 15k, 20k, and marathon.

No-Potato Veggie Soup   Victoria Mitchell

I N G R E D I E N T S

1 large onion

4 c. chopped zucchini

1 cube chicken stock or 1 tsp. chicken stock powder

1 cube vegetable stock or 1 tsp. vegetable stock powder

1 packet of chicken noodle soup

1 tsp. curry powder

2-3/4 c. milk

Brown onion in a little oil. Put onion, zucchini, chicken stock, vegetable stock, chicken noodle soup, curry powder, and water into pot.

Simmer for 30 minutes. Blend until smooth. Add milk and heat without boiling. Salt and pepper to taste.

NOTES FROM THE CHEF: I'm a big soup fan as I grew up in Tolmie near the snow fields in Oz (yes, we get snow!) and loved to eat a hot bowl (or many) of soup with a big roll.

> Victoria Mitchell is an Australian steeplechase champion, and she also won the 2005 NCAA steeplechase title for Butler University. She has run 9:30.84 for the 3,000m steeplechase, and has represented Australia at the Commonwealth Games and World Championships.

Butternut Squash Soup   Anna Willard

I N G R E D I E N T S

1 medium-sized white onion, chopped
2-3 garlic cloves, minced
1 carrot, chopped
1 celery stalk, chopped
2 tbsp. olive oil
1 medium-sized butternut squash, cubed
1 apple (I use Granny Smith), chopped
32 oz. low sodium organic vegetable broth
1/8 c. maple syrup
1/2 tsp. Allspice
1 tsp. cinnamon
1/2 tsp. nutmeg
1/4 c. pine nuts, toasted
1/2 tbsp. cream per serving

Anna Willard won the 3,000m steeplechase at the 2007 NCAA Outdoor Track & Field Championships and finished second in that event at the 2007 USA Outdoor Track & Field Championships.

Begin by chopping all vegetables. In a large soup pot, combine onion, garlic, carrot, celery, and oil over medium heat. Sauté until onions become translucent—about five minutes. Make sure to stir frequently as to coat the vegetables with the oil.

Next, add squash, apple, and broth. Turn up the heat to high, until broth begins to boil. Reduce to medium-low heat and simmer for 15-20 minutes, covered. Stir occasionally.

Check to see if squash chunks are soft. If so, remove from heat and with a hand blender, blend until smooth. Be careful, the soup will be *very* hot. If you don't have a hand blender, divide the soup into two or three portions and blend in a regular blender once the soup has cooled a bit.

Once smooth, stir in maple syrup and spices. Note: Only use pure maple syrup! If you do not have pure maple syrup, you could substitute brown sugar or molasses or just forgo it altogether, because the butternut squash will be plenty sweet on its own.

Garnish with toasted pine nuts and a swirl of cream or crème fraise.

The soup is fantastic served with warm homemade bread. I love to make whole wheat rolls to accompany it, and perhaps serve it with a spinach-chicken-cherry-walnut-gorgonzola salad. It's a very healthy and hearty meal.

NOTES FROM THE CHEF: This recipe is adapted from a Cooking Light recipe I got online. However, I have tweaked the ingredients and proportions so much over time that I like to call it my own now. I love experimental cooking and baking—I encourage everyone to make alterations to this recipe to fit their individual needs and desires.

Pumpkin Peanut Butter Soup

Amby Burfoot

I N G R E D I E N T S

1 small, organic, free-range, backyard, sustainable, hand-crafted pumpkin (or 1 large can pumpkin)

1 jar 100% all-natural peanut butter (don't even look at Skippy's)

Red pepper flakes

6 other random herbs/spices

Carefully cut pumpkin and remove soft pumpkin "meat," causing as little pain as possible to pumpkin. Strain seeds from mash in middle, and roast gently in oven for your daily granola mix. Recycle pumpkin "shell" as Halloween decoration, then candle holder, then (when disgustingly rotten) toss into compost pile.

Microwave pumpkin meat for, oh, about four minutes. If that doesn't work, try six. (I have only exploded two microwave ovens this way, so it's a relatively safe experiment.)

Transfer cooked pumpkin to saucepan, turn burner to "simmer," and add water until you achieve that perfect, gloopy consistency. This can only be determined by bending your ear very close to the saucepan. When it sounds like the early stages of a Mount Vesuvius eruption, all is well.

Add several brimming tablespoons of peanut butter. Then add more. Peanut butter is good for you. "It'll stick to your ribs," my grandfather always used to say, and he was a goober farmer in Virginia—no kidding. Continue to simmer your soup.

Stand five feet from stove and toss pepper flakes in general direction of saucepan. You won't score many "hits," which is precisely the point, as this is the only way to prevent over-pepperizing your soup. At least it's the only thing that works for me. On the other hand, you don't want to under-pepperize either. Red pepper is full of capsaicin, which cures most human ailments, especially runner's knee. Rumors of death by red pepper are urban myth, and contain no truth.

Add brown sugar "to taste" (see below). Yes, I know sugar is an instrument of the Devil. It's also a vigorous athlete's prefered fuel. Like you, I am puzzled by this paradox. Like you, I wish life was more logical. Fairer would be good, too.

Add additional herbs and spices "to taste." Most recipe books don't define this vague term, but I'm a better chef than they are, so I'm going to help you out here. "To taste," literally translated, means "until it tastes really fine to *your* sophisticated palate." Don't worry about anyone else. You'll probably have to eat most of the gloop yourself anyway. Other people are such cowards, aren't they?

> NOTES FROM THE CHEF: This is my favorite soup for the cold winter months. It's especially great for large-group entertainment, when you invite friends over to raucous parties built around major TV presentations such as the Millrose Games, USA Cross Country Championships, Hawaii Ironman reruns or, when desperate, the Super Bowl or Academy Awards. The recipe is also a lot of fun to prepare, due to the combination amusement/fright on your partner's face when he/she/it realizes you're not following any directions and basically have no clue what you're doing.

Amby Burfoot is the 1968 Boston Marathon champion and has a marathon best of 2:14:28.

Hearty Minestrone

I N G R E D I E N T S

1 pound ground turkey

1/2 c. chopped celery

1/2 c. chopped onion

1/2 tsp. garlic (minced)

1 can (28 oz.) crushed tomatoes

1 can (16 oz.) kidney beans, drained

1 can (15 oz.) garbanzo beans, drained

2 c. tomato juice

1 can (15 oz.) tomato sauce

1 can (14 oz.) beef broth

3 medium carrots, chopped

1 medium zucchini, sliced

1 tbsp. Italian seasoning

1 tsp. salt

1/8 tsp. pepper

1/2 c. water

1 c. whole wheat ziti

Cook turkey, celery, onion, and garlic over medium heat in a large soup pot until meat is cooked. Drain.

Stir in tomatoes, beans, tomato juice, tomato sauce, broth, carrots, zucchini, Italian seasoning, salt, and pepper. Bring to a boil, reduce heat, cover and simmer for 30-35 minutes.

In another pot, boil pasta until tender, then drain. Combine water and pasta with soup and simmer for five minutes. Serve and enjoy.

NOTES FROM THE CHEF: This is one of my favorites that my wife, Sarah Sell, makes. Add some garlic bread and a salad for a good meal.

Brian Sell is a 2008 U.S. Olympian in the marathon; he finished third at the 2008 U.S. Olympic Marathon Trials in New York City.

Spinach and Fruit Salad   Lisa Galaviz

I N G R E D I E N T S

Baby spinach

Sliced strawberries

Blueberries

Raspberries

Red grapes

Pine nuts

Raspberry vinaigrette dressing

Mix all of the ingredients. Choose quantities to suit your taste. Prepare salad immediately before you plan to eat.

NOTES FROM THE CHEF: This recipe comes from my aunt Mary Fallini in Hailey, Idaho, who graciously took in my two teammates and me for a month of great summer training!

Lisa Galaviz is the 2006 USA steeplechase champion and she set an American record of 9:28.75 in the steeplechase in 2007.

Secret Salad   Joan Nesbit Mabe

I N G R E D I E N T S

1 c. cottage cheese

2 tbsp. raisins

2 tbsp. salted sunflower seeds

1 small Granny Smith apple, cut up

1/2 banana, sliced

1/2 c. pineapple tidbits (and the juice poured over the entire salad)

Chopped dried apricots or dried cranberries, or whatever fruit is in season (optional)

1/4 c. cranberry juice

Start with the cottage cheese (high or lowfat, depending on your preference) and mix in the raisins, sunflower seeds,

NOTES FROM THE CHEF: In my serious running days, I consumed this salad for lunch every day for about 12 years.

apple, banana, pineapple, and the pineapple juice.

Add dried apricots, dried cranberries, or any other fruit that is in season.

Pour the cranberry juice over everything and mix thoroughly before eating.

Joan Nesbit Mabe is 1996 U.S. Olympian in the 10,000m. She earned a bronze medal in the 3,000m at the 1996 World Indoor Track & Field Championships.

Main Dishes

Barbecue Chicken Pizza · Annie Bersagel

INGREDIENTS

1 tbsp. honey

1 package dry yeast

1 c. warm water (100 to 110*)

1 c. all-purpose flour

1 c. spelt flour

1/4 c. salt

2 skinless, boneless chicken breasts

2 small red onions

1-1/2 c. barbecue sauce

2 c. grated Jarlsberg or mozzarella cheese

To make crust, mix honey, yeast, and water in a large bowl and let sit for 15 minutes, or until mixture is bubbly. Add flour and salt, and mix until dough is formed. Knead dough on a floured surface for about six minutes, adding more flour as needed. Return dough to bowl, cover with a dish towel and let rise for about 45 minutes.

Preheat oven to 400°. Brush chicken breasts with one-half cup of barbecue sauce and bake in large casserole dish with parchment paper (or cooking spray) for 15-20 minutes. Slice onions into rings and bake alongside chicken for last 10 minutes of cooking time.

Turn up oven to 500°. After dough has risen, roll thinly on cooking sheet lined with parchment paper (or cooking spray). Bake crust for five to seven minutes, or until it begins to brown. Remove crust from oven and spread with remaining barbecue sauce. Slice cooked chicken crosswise and layer on top of crust, along with onions and cheese. Return pizza to oven for another five to seven minutes, or until cheese begins to bubble.

Serve pizza with sour cream for dipping or spread on top (a Norwegian tradition) and a fresh salad.

30

Annie Bersagel was an eight-time All-American for Wake Forest University. She is the 2006 USA Half Marathon champion. In 2006, she moved to Norway to study at the University of Oslo on a Fulbright scholarship.

NOTES FROM THE CHEF: This pizza has become a Friday night favorite, even though it takes a little effort to find barbecue sauce in Norway! Time-saving tips: let the dough rise while you are out for a run and set the chicken and onions in the oven before you jump in the shower.

Thai Chicken Pizza Charlie Gruber

I N G R E D I E N T S

1 pizza dough

3/4 c. duck or plum sauce

1/2 tsp. red pepper flakes

1 10 oz. bag shredded provolone or Monterey Jack cheese (about 2 c.)

1/2 red bell pepper, cored, seeded, and thinly sliced

1 tbsp. vegetable oil

2 tbsp. soy sauce

1 rounded tbsp. smooth peanut butter

2 tsp. hot sauce

2 tsp. grill seasoning

4 chicken breast cutlets (about 1/2 lb.)

2 tbsp. honey

2 tbsp. cider vinegar

1/4 seedless cucumber, peeled and cut into matchsticks

4 scallions, white and green parts, chopped

1 c. bean sprouts

A palmful of fresh cilantro, chopped

1/4 c. chopped roasted peanuts

Preheat the oven to 425°. Form the pizza crust on a pizza pan or cookie sheet. Top it with duck or plum sauce, spreading it around like you would pizza sauce. Sprinkle the pizza with some red pepper flakes, then top it with the cheese and bell peppers. Bake until golden and bubbly, 15 to 17 minutes.

In a small bowl, combine the vegetable oil, soy sauce, and peanut butter with the hot sauce and grill seasoning. Use the microwave to loosen up the peanut butter if it is too cold to blend into sauce—10 seconds ought to do it. Coat the chicken evenly with the mixture and let it stand for 10 minutes. Preheat the grill pan or nonstick skillet over medium-high heat. Cook the chicken cutlets for two to three minutes on each side, or until firm. Slice the chicken into very thin strips.

While the chicken cooks, mix the honey and vinegar in a bowl. Add the cucumber and turn to coat in the dressing.

When the pizza comes out of the oven, top it with the chicken, scallions, sprouts, and cilantro. Drain the cucumbers and scatter them over the pizza. Garnish the pizza with the peanuts. Slice and serve. Makes two to four servings.

Charlie Gruber was a 2004 U.S. Olympian at 1,500m. The former KU standout also won the 2004 USA 4k Cross Country title.

Spinach Pie

INGREDIENTS

1 lb. pizza dough (regular, whole wheat and herb are available at Trader Joe's)

1 10 oz. box frozen spinach leaves (or approximately 1 lb. bag of fresh spinach, boiled and drained)

1 4 oz. can sliced black olives

1 clove garlic, minced (optional)

1/2 c. shredded cheese (cheddar, Jack, mozzarella, or crumbled feta—also optional)

4 tbsp. olive oil

Salt and pepper to taste

Preheat oven to 400°. Prepare spinach according to instructions on package. Once cooked, squeeze excess water out using a colander. Set aside.

Heat olive oil in skillet over medium heat, add drained spinach, olives, garlic, salt, and pepper. Sauté about five minutes. Remove from heat and set aside.

Prepare pizza dough according to directions on package, roll out into 12-inch circle. Flour a baking sheet and place dough on sheet. Transfer spinach mixture onto one half of the dough, leaving enough room near the edge to seal it (one-half inch).

Place cheese on top of spinach and fold over the other half of the dough. Use the tines of a fork and press the edges together to seal it. Do not poke holes in the dough.

Bake for 10 minutes.

For easier serving, let cool for a few minutes, then cut in half. I enjoy experimenting with this by adding other vegetables (broccoli, mushrooms, carrots), tomato sauce, or tofu.

A 2004 U.S. Olympian at 5,000m, Jonathon Riley is also a three-time USA Indoor 3,000m champion. He won the 2001 NCAA Outdoor 5,000m title for Stanford.

NOTES FROM THE CHEF: This is a recipe I put together myself, based on the spinach pies I would get at an Italian restaurant when I was a kid. This is also good cold, and it is easily packable for lunch or trips. Just wrap it in foil.

Pizza Pie

Kristen Nicolini Lehmkuhle

I N G R E D I E N T S

16 oz. spaghetti

1/2 c. milk

3/4 tsp. garlic powder

1/2 tsp. salt

2 eggs

3 c. lowfat shredded mozzarella

2 cans of diced tomatoes

4 tbsp. tomato paste

1-1/2 tsp. oregano

Sliced turkey pepperoni

Preheat oven to 400°. Break spaghetti in half, cook and drain. Beat eggs, milk, one cup of the cheese, and garlic powder. Add spaghetti.

Mix together the diced tomatoes and tomato paste.

Coat a 9x13-inch pan with cooking spray. Use some of the tomato sauce to cover the bottom of the pan; this keeps the dish from drying out.

Add spaghetti mixture to the pan. Cook for 15 minutes at 400°.

Remove pan from oven and lower oven temperature to 350°. Spread the remainder of the sauce, oregano, the remaining two cups of cheese, and sliced turkey pepperoni to the top of the spaghetti.

Cook for an additional 30 minutes at 350°. Let stand for five minutes before serving.

Kristen Nicolini Lehmkuhle was a member of Villanova's cross country team which won the 1998 NCAA Cross Country Championship. She was a three-time high school national champion, and more recently finished fifth at the 2008 USA Half Marathon Championship.

NOTES FROM THE CHEF: My mom used to make this when I was in high school and we hosted team dinners. I started making it when I was in college for the same reason. I still use this recipe when I have a lot of hungry runners to entertain. It feeds a lot and is easy to make.

Teriyaki Chicken and Vegetables

Scott Bauhs

INGREDIENTS

1 lb. boneless chicken breast
1/2 c. teriyaki sauce
2 tbsp. brown sugar
2 c. broccoli
1 c. carrots, sliced
1 c. snow peas
1/2 onion, sliced
1 c. white rice

Additional teriyaki or soy sauce for extra seasoning, if desired

Slice chicken into bite-sized pieces, combine with brown sugar and teriyaki sauce, and let sit for at least 20 minutes.

Slice vegetables into bite-sized pieces and set aside.

Preheat a pan on medium high and pour chicken and sauce into the pan. Cover and cook for five minutes.

Bring one cup of water to boil in a pan, add vegetables, and cook on medium high for five minutes.

Start rice in a rice cooker.

Combine chicken and sauce with vegetables, cover and cook on medium heat for five more minutes.

Serve in a bowl over rice. Add extra teriyaki or soy sauce, if desired.

NOTES FROM THE CHEF: Teriyaki sauce is a wonderful thing that makes just about anything taste good. It is also a staple in my weekly foods. This recipe can be altered to include beef, pork, fish or tofu, and the vegetables can be changed or taken out as well.

Scott Bauhs is an NCAA DII national champion and All-American for California State University, Chico. He has run a 1:03:04 half marathon and he represented the U.S. at the 2008 World Cross Country Championships.

Vegetable Calzone

Paul Pilkington

INGREDIENTS

1 box frozen chopped spinach (thaw and squeeze out excess water)
1/2 c. sliced mushrooms
2 garlic cloves
1/4 c. brown sugar
1/4 c. olive oil
1/4 c. parmesan cheese
1/4 c. asiago cheese
1 tomato, chopped
1 red pepper, chopped
1 loaf Rhodes bread, thawed

Preheat oven to 350°. Saute spinach, mushrooms and garlic in oil until mushrooms are soft. Stir in brown sugar, cheeses, tomato, and red pepper.

Roll dough into a rectangle. Put filling on one half of the dough. Fold other half over and pinch the edges together to seal. Cut a few small slits in top to allow steam to escape.

Bake on cookie sheet sprayed with Pam for 15 minutes, until browned. Brush top with butter and serve.

Paul Pilkington won the 1990 Houston Marathon, the 1994 Los Angeles Marathon, and the 1992 USA 20k title. He represented the U.S. at the 1995 World Outdoor Track & Field Championships.

Veggie and Chicken Stir Fry   Kara and Adam Goucher

I N G R E D I E N T S

1 tbsp. peanut oil

1 tbsp. minced garlic

1 tbsp. sesame seeds

1/2 c. dry brown rice

1 4-6 oz. package refrigerated stir fry noodles

1 lb. boneless and skinless chicken breast, cut into thin strips

1 11.5 oz. bottle classic stir fry sauce—we like House of Tsang, but any brand will do

1 package or about 9 oz. bean sprouts

1 large carrot, peeled and sliced

3-4 white mushrooms, washed and sliced

1/2 medium red onion, sliced

1/2 red pepper, washed and sliced

1 zucchini, washed, halved lengthwise, and cut into strips

1 head of broccoli, washed and florets cut up

2 tbsp. of water

Salt and pepper to taste

Kara Goucher was a three-time NCAA champion for the University of Colorado. She won a bronze medal in the 10,000m at the 2007 World Outdoor Track & Field Championships.

The hardest part of this meal is the preparation. Get your brown rice started on the stove or in your rice cooker. While it is cooking, wash and slice all of your vegetables. Put them all together in a large bowl. Then slice the chicken and move it to the side.

Heat the tablespoon of peanut oil in your wok on medium high heat. When it is hot, add the garlic and the sesame seeds. Let them simmer in the oil for about a minute or two.

When the garlic has started to turn a golden brown, add your bowl of vegetables. You will want to stir them every minute or so, allowing them to cook evenly. Sprinkle the vegetables with salt and pepper. After sautéing them

for about five to six minutes, add a few tablespoons of the stir fry sauce. You don't want the veggies drowning in the sauce; you just want them to be lightly coated. Stir fry the veggies for another minute or two and then remove them from the wok and pour them back into the big bowl.

Return the wok to the heat and add your chicken. If you wok is hot, you won't need to add more oil. Season your chicken with salt and pepper. When the chicken begins to look done, add three tablespoons of your stir fry sauce. Cook the chicken for a minute more, and then push the chicken to the outside of the wok.

(Continued on page 36)

Veggie and Chicken Stir Fry, continued   Adam and Kara Goucher

Turn your wok down to medium or medium low heat, and add the noodles to the center of the wok. Put two tablespoons of water on the noodles and gently move them around until they begin to break up. This will take a few minutes. When the noodles begin to break up, add about two tablespoons of the stir fry sauce to the noodles and chicken.

Once the noodles have broken up and are pliable, mix in the cooked brown rice. Once again, add two tablespoons of the stir fry sauce. Turn your wok down to low heat. Mix the chicken, noodles, and rice.

Once they are well mixed, return the veggies to the wok. Mix everything together. You may need to add more stir fry sauce to the wok. You can use half or a whole bottle, it depends on how flavorful you wish to have it. Adam and I usually use three-quarters of a bottle.

Once the chicken, rice, noodles, and veggies are well mixed and flavored to your liking, remove from heat and serve. This meal feeds about four to five people, although when Adam and I eat it, it feeds us each a large dinner and a small lunch the next day.

Adam and I often eat this in our sweats, just out of cereal bowls. But you can dress is up for company by serving it with chopsticks and a crisp bottle of white wine. Trust me, it sounds more difficult than it is. Enjoy!

A 2000 U.S. Olympian at 5,000m, Adam Goucher has run 13:10.00 for that distance. He has won national titles at the high school, NCAA, and senior levels.

NOTES FROM THE CHEF: This is one of Adam's absolute favorite recipes that I make. We eat it once a week.

We used to go to the New Seasons Market and order wok bowls. One day, I thought to myself, "I could make this!" And so I tried it at home and it was delicious. It's a good healthy meal, giving you good carbs, lots of veggies, and lean meat. It takes a bit of time to prep all of the veggies, but once that is done it is pretty easy.

—Kara Goucher

Thai Chicken and Vegetables with Coconut   Jo Pavey

I N G R E D I E N T S

5 chicken breasts

150g/5 oz. mangetout (snap peas)

150g/5 oz. baby corn, chopped into pieces

2 medium red bell peppers, chopped

400 ml./13.5 oz. tin of coconut milk

2 tbsp. lime juice

2 green chilies, deseeded and finely chopped

2 medium onions, finely chopped

4 tbsp. fresh coriander leaves, finely chopped

2 tbsp. olive oil

3 cloves garlic, crushed

1 tsp. cumin

2 tsp. turmeric

Cut the chicken into small bite-sized pieces and put aside.

Heat the oil in a large frying pan or wok, then add the chicken and stir fry until slightly browned.

Add the finely chopped onions, garlic, and green chilies, and stir fry for two to three minutes.

Now add the mangetout (snap peas), baby corn, and red pepper, and stir fry for an additional five minutes.

Then stir in the cumin and turmeric so that it is thoroughly mixed in.

Now pour in the coconut milk, and lime juice, mix in and simmer for about eight minutes, until reduced.

Add the chopped coriander leaves and simmer for another two minutes.

Serve with basmati rice. Serves four.

Jo Pavey finished fifth in the 5,000m at the 2004 Olympic Games and fourth in the 10,000m at the 2007 World Outdoor Track & Field Championships. She has run 14:39.96 for 5,000m.

Smothered Burrito   Cheryl (Bridges Flanagan) Treworgy

I N G R E D I E N T S

Canned black beans

Flour tortillas

Cooked rice

Shredded Monterey cheese

Las Palma Green Enchilada Sauce

Chopped lettuce

Tomatoes

Cooked shredded chicken

Sour cream and/or guacamole

In 1971, Cheryl Treworgy, then Cheryl Bridges, became the first woman to break 2:50 in the marathon, running 2:49:40. Treworgy was also a member of five World Cross Country teams.

Optional ingredients which add flavor: Sautéed chopped onion, Sazon Goya seasoning, salsa

Heat black beans with onions and some Goya seasoning (to taste). On flour tortillas, layer beans, rice, cheese, and chicken. Fold in sides and flip over.

Pour on green enchilada sauce, sprinkle on cheese and heat in microwave until cheese melts.

Pile on lettuce, tomatoes, sour cream and guacamole or salsa. Green enchilada sauce is milder than red and harder to find, but worth the hunt.

Flanagan/Edwards Fajitas

I N G R E D I E N T S

1 can black beans, drained

2 c. shredded cheddar cheese

2 c. chopped lettuce

2 c. salsa or chopped tomatoes

1/2 large yellow onion, sliced

1 green pepper, sliced

1 red pepper, sliced

1-2 avocados

1-2 lb. chopped chicken, steak, or turkey burger (depending on preference for the night)

1 package whole wheat tortillas

2 tbsp. olive oil

1 tbsp. lime juice

Note: While cooking, I add salt, pepper, and garlic and onion powder to taste.

First, get all of the condiments ready by chopping and slicing the lettuce, tomatoes, onions, and peppers.

Next, put two tablespoons of olive oil on skillet over medium heat. Add the green and red peppers, onion, salt, and pepper. Saute until softened, then add desired meat, garlic, and onion powder. Stir occasionally until meat is fully cooked. Let simmer until all other ingredients are ready.

To warm the tortillas, preheat oven to 200°. Wrap tortillas in damp paper towel and cover in aluminum foil. Heat for 15 minutes.

For yummy guacamole, scoop out the avocado flesh from the peel, and lightly mash with fork. Add chopped tomato or salsa, the lime juice, and a dash of onion powder. Stir.

Once everything is cooked, lay out all of the ingredients in separate bowls and serve buffet style. This is super easy and can be cooked up in 15-20 minutes. Enjoy!

Shalane Flanagan is a 2004 U.S. Olympian at 5,000m. In 2007, she set an American 5,000m record of 14:44.80. In 2008, she set an American 10,000m record of 30:34.49.

NOTES FROM THE CHEF: My husband, Steve Edwards, and I cook this at least once a week. We crave Mexican food most of the time, so we jazzed up this recipe to meet our cravings and nutritional needs.

Thousand Hills Cattle Co. Carne Asada (for Fajitas) Carrie Tollefson

I N G R E D I E N T S

1/2 bunch cilantro, chopped

4 limes, juiced

1 tsp. cumin

1 tsp. granulated garlic

1 tsp. paprika

4 cloves garlic

3-4 lb. 100% grass-fed skirt/flank steak, cleaned

Place all ingredients into a seal-lock bag, making sure to turn the bag regularly so the marinade penetrates both sides evenly.

Remove the meat from the bag, place on heated broiler or grill, and cook to medium rare.

Thinly slice and serve! Accompany with your favorite fajita toppings, including, grilled onion, fresh tomato, avocado, sautéed peppers, or just rolled in a warm tortilla. Enjoy!

Carrie Tollefson is a 2004 U.S. Olympian at 1,500m. She has won U.S. national titles in the 1,500m, 3,000m, and in cross country. Tollefson was a five-time individual NCAA champion for Villanova.

NOTES FROM THE CHEF: I discovered this recipe when Chef Rachel Rubin came to my home and taught me how to cook Thousand Hills Cattle Company beef. The company provides me with free beef, which is a great iron source. After I was anemic one year, they said they couldn't have their Minnesota Olympian running on empty. I would much rather eat good food which is high in nutrients than take supplements—way more fun!

I love to cook, but Chef Rubin came over to give me a few ideas and explain how to heat the beef to a certain point, before it gets too hard. It doesn't take much time at all to cook because it is so lean. It's very good, and it's sold everywhere.

Enchilada Casserole Jen Rhines

I N G R E D I E N T S

1 tbsp. canola oil

1 small red onion

1 lb. ground sirloin

Cumin to taste

Red Pepper flakes to taste

1 15 oz. can black beans

1 15 oz. can yellow corn

1 16 oz. can tomato sauce

1 10-15 oz. can red enchilada sauce

1 2 oz. can sliced black olives (optional)

8-12 flour tortillas

8 oz. Mexican cheese blend

Preheat oven to 350°. Heat canola oil on medium heat in skillet. Add onion and cook until translucent. Add ground beef and cook until browned. Season the meat with cumin and red pepper to your taste.

Mix tomato and enchilada sauce together in large bowl. Drain and rinse the corn and black beans. Add half to two-thirds of the tomato/enchilada sauce mixture to the meat and onions. Add beans, corn, and olives and bring to a boil. Turn heat to low and simmer for eight to 10 minutes.

Lightly grease a 9x13-inch casserole pan. Place tortillas on the bottom and sides of the pan. Add the meat mixture and sprinkle half of the cheese on top. Place tortillas over the meat mixture. Add the rest of the sauce and spread over the top. Sprinkle with the rest of the cheese. Bake for 45-50 minutes.

Serve with guacamole and sour cream.

Jen Rhines is one of the most versatile U.S. distance runners currently competing. She was a 2000 U.S. Olympian at 10,000m and a 2004 U.S. Olympian in the marathon. In 2007, she finished seventh in the 5,000m at the World Outdoor Track & Field Championships.

NOTES FROM THE CHEF: This is what I usually make when I have my Team Running USA teammates over for dinner.

Green Enchiladas

1 lb. chicken

Garlic salt

1 bag shredded reduced-fat cheddar cheese (or Mexican mix)

Approximately 10 medium-sized fat-free flour tortillas

1 small can sliced black olives

1 large can green chile verde enchilada sauce (I like spicy sauce but my sisters use mild)

Preheat oven to 350°. Boil chicken until the juices run clear, then shred and place in bowl. Add half the bag of cheese and half the olives. Mix, and sprinkle with garlic salt to taste. Pour half the jar of sauce into the bowl, and mix until everything is covered.

Place some of the mixture in the middle of a tortilla and roll it up. Place the tortilla in a lightly-greased 9x13-inch glass baking dish. Continue doing this until pan is full. Cover tortillas with remaining enchilada sauce, and sprinkle with more cheese and olives.

Bake for 30 to 35 minutes, until sauce is bubbling and cheese is melted. Serve immediately.

I like to cut up some jalapeños and sprinkle them on top of the enchiladas but apparently this makes me weird and my wife thinks I

NOTES FROM THE CHEF:
This recipe comes from my sisters, Michelle and Merae. It is always a favorite, and it's great to serve with guacamole and chips.

should leave this part out...but jalapeños make you faster, smarter, tougher, and all around a much better person—so this part stays.

I also like to make my own baked chips to go with this. Just get a bag of small corn tortillas, cut them into quarters, lay them on a cookie sheet, and pop them in a 350° oven for 10 minutes or so. Yet another testament to the versatility of the tortilla—the greatest food invention of all time. In 20 years the tortilla should completely overtake bread's role in society.

Josh Cox is a three-time U.S. Olympic Marathon Trials qualifier and a 2:13:55 marathoner.

Grandma D's Goulash

Matt Gabrielson

I N G R E D I E N T S

1/4 lb. small pieces of bacon

1-1/2 lb. hamburger

3 tbsp. onion, chopped

3 tbsp. celery, chopped

3 tbsp. green pepper, chopped

1 small can tomato sauce

1 46 oz. can tomato juice

2 c. dry elbow macaroni

Chili powder to taste

Sugar to taste

Salt and pepper to taste

Brown the bacon. Drain and set aside. Brown the hamburger with the onion, celery, and green pepper. Drain well.

Add the tomato sauce and three-quarters of the can of tomato juice to the hamburger, saving the rest to add it later, as the macaroni will absorb a lot.

In separate large pan, add the elbows to boiling water. Use plenty of water. Stir elbows while adding them, to prevent them from sticking together. Cook until just tender—do not overcook! Drain. Rinse just a little so the tomato sauce will adhere to the starchy elbows. Drain well.

Add the tomato/meat sauce and bacon to the cooked and drained macaroni. Heat it slowly, occasionally stirring carefully.

Season to taste, a little at a time. You can always add more seasoning but you can't remove it! Start with one or one-half of a teaspoon of chili powder, a couple pinches of sugar, and some salt and pepper.

The goulash should be quite juicy. Add the remaining tomato juice as needed. Stir often and carefully while heating. Do not heat on high, as it will stick to the bottom of the pan.

Matt Gabrielson has represented the U.S. at the World Cross Country Championships three times. He finished second at the 2005 USA Half Marathon Championships.

NOTES FROM THE CHEF:
This recipe comes from my Grandma, Doris Gabrielson. She lives two hours from me in Belmond, Iowa. Whenever I go home, she makes enough for me to freeze for about a month. I like to heat it up and eat it after a hard Minnesota winter workout or a long winter run.

Turkey Sweet Potato Shepherd's Pie   Mary Cullen

I N G R E D I E N T S

2-1/2 lb. (approximately 1.15 kg.) sweet potatoes, peeled and cut into 1-inch cubes

2 tbsp. extra virgin olive oil

2 lb./900 g. ground turkey, minced

1 large onion, chopped

2 large carrots, grated

4 celery sticks from the center, chopped

1/2 can red or black kidney beans, drained (optional—to raise mineral and antioxidant content)

4 tbsp. butter (2 if watching fat intake)

2 tbsp. flour

2 c./475 ml. turkey or chicken broth (made from MSG-free chicken stock cubes, such as Kallo)

A few dashes Worcestershire sauce

10 oz./250 g. packet frozen peas

1/3 ripe banana, sliced

A few dashes hot pepper sauce

Sea salt

Pepper, ground

2 c. shredded sharp cheddar cheese*

*Omit if watching your fat intake; save for a treat. You could substitute breadcrumbs, so that you get a nice toasted crumb topping without the fat.

In a large saucepan, combine the sweet potatoes and enough cold water to cover. Bring to a boil, salt the water, and cook until tender, roughly 15 minutes. Drain and set aside, reserving the pot.

While the sweet potatoes cook, preheat the oven to 425° F/220° C. In a deep pan or casserole dish, heat the olive oil, two turns of the pan, over high heat. Add the turkey and cook, breaking up with a spoon. Stir in the onion, carrots, celery, and kidney beans if using (recommended). Season with sea salt and pepper and cook for five minutes.

In a small saucepan, melt two tablespoons of the butter over medium heat. Whisk in the flour for one minute, then whisk in the turkey broth and season with salt, pepper, and the Worcestershire sauce. Simmer for a few minutes until thickened, then stir into the turkey mixture. Stir in the peas and remove from the heat. If you are watching your fat intake, you could make a thickened stock without butter by adding one or two teaspoons of cornflour (cornstarch) directly to the stock, seasoning with salt, pepper, and Worcestershire sauce, heating and then continuing the recipe as written (recommended).

Add the remaining two tablespoons butter to the sweet potato pot and melt over medium low heat. Add the sweet potatoes and banana; season with salt, pepper, and the Worcestershire sauce and mash until combined. (Or, instead of using butter, add a minimal amount of extra virgin olive oil or hemp oil directly into the sweet potatoes and banana, and then season with salt, pepper, and Worcestershire sauce. This reduces the saturated fat content of the dish).

Mary Cullen, a native of Ireland, won the 2006 NCAA 5,000m title for Providence College. She now runs professionally for Reebok.

43

Meatloaf

I N G R E D I E N T S

1-1/2 lb. lean ground beef

1 slightly beaten egg

1/2 c. seasoned dry breadcrumbs

1/4 c. onion, finely chopped

1/3 c. milk

1/4 c. Sweet Baby Ray's Barbecue Sauce (the key ingredient)

3/4 tsp. salt

1/8 tsp. pepper

Preheat oven to 350°. Mix the ground beef, beaten egg, breadcrumbs, chopped onions, milk, barbecue sauce, salt, and pepper. Mix gently but thoroughly. Put mixture into a loaf pan.

Bake for more than an hour. Once done, add more Sweet Baby Ray's Barbecue Sauce to the top and serve.

Jason Hartmann was an All-American distance runner for the University of Oregon. He placed 10th at the 2008 U.S. Olympic Marathon Trials in 2:15:27. Hartmann has represented the U.S. at the World Cross Country Championships and the World Half Marathon Championships.

Sloppy Joes and Sweet Potato Fries   Carrie Messner Vickers

I N G R E D I E N T S

1 lb. lean ground beef

1/2 medium yellow onion, chopped

1 clove garlic, chopped

1/4 c. green bell pepper, chopped

1/4 c. yellow bell pepper, chopped

1 small can of tomato sauce

1/2 tsp. garlic powder

1 tsp. dry yellow mustard

1/4 c. ketchup or barbecue sauce
(barbecue sauce makes it spicier)

3 tsp. brown sugar

2 tsp. apple cider vinegar

2 tsp. chili powder

Dash of red pepper flakes for spice

Salt and pepper to taste

Buns of your choice

To make sloppy joes, brown the beef in a pan, and drain most of fat. Add onion, garlic, and peppers. Cook on medium heat for about five minutes.

Add the rest of the ingredients. Mix well and let simmer for about 15 minutes.

Serve over toasted buns, nice and sloppy. Be sure to get your fingers all messy as its part of the sloppy goodness!

I N G R E D I E N T S

2 large sweet potatoes

2-3 tbsp. walnut oil (lots of good omegas!)

1 tbsp. Spice Islands Mesquite Seasoning

Dash of cinnamon

Dash of paprika

Salt and pepper

To make sweet potato fries, preheat oven to 375°. Cut two sweet potatoes in half, then into half-inch strips.

Place strips out on a cooking sheet and drizzle with walnut oil. Sprinkle with mesquite seasoning, paprika, and cinnamon. Be sure to use a spatula to flip the potatoes, so you can get both sides. Salt and pepper to taste.

Bake for about 20 minutes, or until done. Be sure to flip them over halfway through.

Carrie Messner Vickers finished fourth in the 3,000m steeplechase at the 2004 U.S. Olympic Trials, before the steeplechase became an Olympic event. Messner Vickers represented the U.S. in the steeplechase at the 2005 World Outdoor Track & Field Championships and was the #1 ranked steepler in the U.S. in 2006.

NOTES FROM THE CHEF: I love food that tastes good and makes me happy, which means I like a lot of childhood favorites. This is one of my favorite post-long run dinners. I don't usually cook with recipes, as both of my parents grew up in restaurants, and my grandfather's advice on cooking was to "Get rid of the cookbook," so it's a little of this and that. Both recipes are a combined effort of trial and error and practice on my husband. I love to cook and try new things, but this is a simple standby that everyone loves, and it's very quick, which is nice when you've just finished a long workout and you're super hungry!

Chipotle Sloppy Joes   Matt Tegenkamp

I N G R E D I E N T S

1 lb. ground beef

1/4 c. chopped onion

3/4 c. ketchup

1/2 c. frozen corn

1/2 c. canned black beans, rinsed and drained

1/2 c. tomato sauce

1-2 tsp. chipotle chile pepper

1/2 tsp. ground cumin

1/4 c. chopped fresh cilantro

1/4 tsp. salt

1/4 tsp. black pepper

Brown ground beef with onion in large nonstick skillet over medium heat for eight to 10 minutes, or until beef is no longer pink, breaking beef up into three-quarter inch crumbles. Pour off drippings.

Stir in ketchup, corn, beans, tomato sauce, chipotle pepper, and cumin; bring to a boil. Reduce heat; simmer for five minutes, stirring often. Stir in cilantro, salt, and black pepper.

Place cheese slice on bottom of bun, then place beef mixture on top and enjoy. This goes great with mashed potatoes and a side salad.

This is adapted from a recipe which originally appeared in *The Healthy Beef Cookbook*.

Matt Tegenkamp finished fourth in the 5,000m at the 2007 World Outdoor Track & Field Championships. He set an American record of 8:07.07 in the two-mile in 2007. Tegenkamp also won the 2007 and 2008 USA Indoor 3,000m titles.

INGREDIENTS

- 2 tbsp. corn oil
- 1 large onion, chopped
- 4 large garlic cloves, chopped
- 1 tbsp. ground cumin
- 1 tsp. dried oregano
- 1/2 tsp. dried crushed red pepper
- 1 lb. boneless skinless chicken breasts, cut into 1-inch pieces
- 3 15 oz. cans cannellini beans (white kidney beans)
- 2 c. canned chicken broth
- 1 7 oz. can diced green chilies
- 1/2 c. whipping cream
- Cheddar cheese, grated
- Salt and pepper to taste

Heat oil in Dutch oven over medium heat. Add onion, garlic, cumin, oregano, and dried red pepper. Sauté for five minutes. Push onion to one side of the pan. Season chicken with salt and pepper and add to pan. Sauté chicken for approximately five minutes.

Drain beans, reserving half of the bean liquid. Add beans, broth, chilies, cream, and reserved bean liquid to chicken. Simmer until chicken is tender and cooked through, about 10 minutes. (You can also prepare this a day in advance—just refrigerate and reheat the next day.)

Pour chili into bowls. Top with cheese.

NOTES FROM THE CHEF:
This recipe is from my mom, Teresa Hasay. We serve it with brown rice and vegetables. It can also be cooked in a Crock Pot so that it's ready as soon as track practice is over!

Jordan Hasay won a silver medal in the 1,500m at the 2007 World Youth Championships. She won the 2005 Foot Locker Cross Country title, the 2007 and 2008 USA Junior Cross Country titles, the 2006 USA Junior 3,000m title, and the 2007 USA Junior 1,500m title.

INGREDIENTS

2 cans kidney beans (dark red)
2 cans chili beans (pink)
2 cans black beans
2 cans pinto beans
2 cans garbanzo beans
Tomatoes—fresh from the garden or a big can of diced or stewed ones
1 can corn
2 green peppers, chopped
2 onions, chopped
8 mushrooms, chopped
2-4 jalapeños, finely chopped
1 lb. hamburger or ground turkey
Chili powder to taste
Cumin to taste
Garlic powder to taste
Black pepper to taste
Red pepper to taste
Cajun spice to taste
Tabasco sauce to taste
Beer (optional)

Notes on the ingredients: You can stick with one kind of bean, but my preference is to include a variety. As for the spices or the "flavor," that will depend on how hot you can tolerate your chili. I add all of the spices listed, and take a big swig of a beer before pouring the rest in. The beer is optional, but it adds a little zest. I use generous amounts of the spices initially, and then as needed at the end.

Drain all of the beans, except for the kidney beans. Combine all of the beans with the tomatoes, corn, and spices in a crock pot, and cook on medium or high heat. At the same time, brown the vegetables in olive oil, and then put them into the pot.

Cook the meat until done. Drain the fat and juice, and then add it to the crock pot. Cook on high heat until the chili starts to bubble,

then drop it down to a lower temperature and let it sit for a couple of hours, stirring a few times. After a couple of hours, take a few tastes, and then add additional flavor as desired.

I usually cook the chili for about three to four hours. The process can be sped up, but the flavors do not get soaked up as well if you're trying to prepare it in 30 minutes.

Serve chili with some shredded cheese and sour cream on top, some nacho chips on the side, and a couple of Coors Lights and enjoy. In addition to hitting the spot by itself, it also goes great on top of nachos, burgers, and hotdogs the next day as well!

> NOTES FROM THE CHEF: I love to cook, and rarely do I cook with actual measurements. I prefer to go by taste and experience. A crock pot is a great thing to cook chili in, but a big pan on the stove works as well. When making chili, I like to make a lot of it so that I can eat it for a few days and then even freeze some for a meal down the road. If making it for one, or for a family meal once, then you will probably want to pare things down a little.

Erik Nedeau won a bronze medal in the 1,500m at the 1995 World Indoor Track & Field Championships, and placed fourth in the 1,500m at the 1996 U.S. Olympic Trials.

African Stew
Rod DeHaven

I N G R E D I E N T S

2 c. red onions, chopped

2 tbsp. peanut oil

1 tsp. cayenne

2 tsp. garlic

3 c. sweet potatoes, chopped

3 c. V8 juice

1 c. apple juice

1 tsp. salt

1 tsp. fresh ginger root

1/2 c. peanut butter

2 c. tomatoes, chopped

Chicken (optional)

Cilantro

In a large stew pot, sauté the onions, peanut oil, cayenne, and garlic for about five minutes. Then add the sweet potatoes, V8 juice, apple juice, salt, and ginger root. Let it simmer until the sweet potatoes are slightly tender.

Add the peanut butter, stir well, and let it simmer for approximately 20 more minutes.

Serve with fresh cilantro and chopped tomatoes. Chicken can also be added.

This is adapted from a recipe which originally appeared in the *Moosewood Cookbook*.

Rod DeHaven is the 2000 U.S. Olympic Marathon Trials champion, and he represented the U.S. at the 2000 Olympic Games.

Chicken Chili
Erin Donohue

I N G R E D I E N T S

2 packages of McCormick Hot Chili Seasoning Mix

2 lb. of Perdue or Tyson ground chicken

2 cans of Busch's Black Beans

2 cans of diced tomatoes

Follow directions on the back of the McCormick package. Serve with cheese and tortilla chips.

NOTES FROM THE CHEF: I'm not a big fan of cooking. I mostly just like eating. But this recipe is very easy and provides lots of leftovers.

Erin Donohue was an All-American and ACC champion for the University of North Carolina. She represented the U.S. in the 1,500m at the 2007 World Outdoor Track & Field Championships.

INGREDIENTS

1/4 c. tomato paste

1/4 c. apple cider vinegar

1-1/2 tsp. Worcestershire sauce

1 tbsp. paprika

1-1/2 tsp. dried herbs — any combination of thyme, oregano, and rosemary

3 lb. English-cut short ribs

1 tbsp. plus 1 tsp. kosher salt, divided

1 large yellow onion, thinly sliced

1 lb. red potatoes, unpeeled and finely diced

Freshly ground black pepper

1 tbsp. chopped fresh parsley leaves

First, mix the tomato paste, cider vinegar, Worcestershire sauce, paprika, and dried herbs. Use a large bowl.

Season the ribs with one tablespoon of the kosher salt. On a large, hot griddle over medium-high heat, sear the meat on all sides. When the meat is browned, add it to the bowl with the paste and this mixture until the meat is coated. Once this is done, wrap the meat with a large piece of heavy aluminum foil, and put this package into a metal pan. This should go into a cold oven on the middle rack. With the meat inside, set the oven to 250°.

After four hours, take the meat back out and drain it. You can do this by carefully puncturing the foil and catching the drippings in a heatproof container such as a Pyrex glass. Cool the drained liquid in the refrigerator until it separates, which may take about an hour. Then transfer the liquid to the freezer and leave it there until the fat on the top of the glass has solidified (roughly another hour). Meanwhile, if you're serving the stew the same day, you can let the ribs sit while the liquid is cooling; if it's being served the next day, put them in the refrigerator.

Take the liquid out of the freezer and remove the fat cap at the top. Put one tablespoon in a saucepan and place that over medium heat until the fat has re-melted. Add the onion and the teaspoon of salt, and move the onions around gently to separate the rings. Cook these onion rings for two or three minutes, stirring now and then, before stirring in the potatoes and a pinch of black pepper. Next, stir in the rest of the liquid from the meat and stir it in. Cover the saucepan tightly and decrease the heat until no heat is leaking out of the lid. Leave this for a half hour, or until the potatoes are fork tender.

Meanwhile, separate the meat from the ribs, and trim any gristle. When the potatoes are done, put the meat in on top, re-cover the saucepan, and cook for another 10 minutes. Sprinkle the parsley on top before serving.

This is adapted from an Alton Brown recipe, which appeared on the "Stew Romance" episode of "Good Eats."

NOTES FROM THE CHEF: This one takes some planning but it is great for a cold winter day when you need a good, hearty meal. I tend to edit most recipes, and this one is great with some Asian flavors. I like to use Hoisin sauce instead of the tomato paste and add some fresh ginger and soy sauce. You can also add whatever vegetables you want. I like to add carrots and cabbage and serve it over rice.

Zika Rea is a two-time U.S. Olympic Marathon Trials qualifier who has represented the U.S. internationally. She is a co-founder of ZAP Fitness.

Macaroni and Cheese

I N G R E D I E N T S

4 oz. thick bacon slices

Vegetable oil

Kosher salt

2 c. elbow macaroni or cavatappi

1-1/2 c. milk

2 tbsp. unsalted butter

2 tbsp. all-purpose flour

4 oz. Gruyère cheese, grated

3 oz. extra sharp cheddar cheese, grated

2 oz blue cheese, such as Roquefort, crumbled

1/4 tsp. freshly ground black pepper

Pinch of nutmeg

2 slices white sandwich bread, crusts removed

2 tbsp. freshly chopped basil leaves

Preheat the oven to 400°. Put a baking rack on top of a sheet pan. Place bacon in single layer on baking rack, and bake for 15 to 20 minutes, until the bacon is crisp. Remove pan from oven, being careful of the hot grease. Line a plate with paper towels, transfer bacon to it, and crumble bacon when it is cool enough to do so.

Boil a pot of water, add some salt, and drizzle in some oil. Pour in the macaroni and follow cooking instructions on package, which will likely be six to eight minutes. Once tender, drain well.

Heat but don't boil the milk in a small saucepan. Melt the butter in a medium pot before adding the flour. Cook this on low heat for two minutes, periodically stirring it with a whisk. Next, add the hot milk and cook for one to two additional minutes, until the mixture is smooth and has thickened. Remove from heat, then add the Gruyère, cheddar, blue cheese, one teaspoon of salt, the one-quarter teaspoon of pepper, and the pinch of nutmeg. Add the macaroni and bacon and stir it well. Split the mixture between two individual size gratin dishes.

Put bread slices into a food processor with a steel blade. Pulse until you have crumbs. Add basil and continue pulsing to combine the two. Add the breadcrumb mixture to the top of the macaroni dishes. Bake for 35 to 40 minutes, or until the sauce bubbles and the macaroni is a little brown on top.

This is adapted from a recipe featured on the Food Network's "Barefoot Contessa" show.

NOTES FROM THE CHEF: I've found this to be simple and pleasing to the whole family and guests. The Gruyère cheese and the bacon give it a smooth and creamy, slightly different taste. I hope you love it as much as the Dillons do!

Patti Dillon was the first American woman to break 2:30 in the marathon. She once held world bests for 5 miles, 10k, 20k, the half marathon, and 30k. She has been inducted into the National Distance Running Hall of Fame.

Macaroni and Cheese

INGREDIENTS

1 lb. box of elbow macaroni
12 oz. white American cheese (roughly 10 individually wrapped slices, if you prefer) broken into 1/4 of the slice size
12 oz. white cheddar cheese, shredded or cut up into thin, small pieces
2 tbsp. butter
1 c. whole milk (if substitute 2% use 3/4 c., if 1% 2/3 c., if skim use 1/2 c.)
Black pepper (optional)

Boil a pot of water for the macaroni. While the water comes to a boil, prepare the cheese, and measure the milk and butter. Add the macaroni to the water when it reaches a rolling boil. Stir regularly to avoid clumping. (You can also add a little oil before boiling the water, if you wish.)

When macaroni is done, strain out the water and return the macaroni to the pot. Add all other ingredients except the black pepper. Stir until everything is fully melted and uniformly mixed. Add pepper to taste, if you wish. (Small amounts go a long way—start with only a teaspoon or so.)

Nate Jenkins, a former NCAA Division II star for UMass-Lowell, finished seventh in the 2008 U.S. Olympic Marathon Trials in 2:14:56.

NOTES FROM THE CHEF: My mom, Tama Vincent, used to make mac and cheese, but when I asked her for a recipe she gave me a look like I was an idiot and said, "It's got macaroni and cheese in it." So the above recipe resulted from experimenting a bit throughout high school and college. Some other good options are to change cheese types—provolone and mozzarella are my other two favorites to mix in. You can also add in chunks of ham—it's not my favorite, but I have friends who love it. I think bits of bacon are better, but not if you use provolone, because it comes out a bit too salty.

Pasta Arrabiata

Sebastian Coe

I N G R E D I E N T S

200 g./7 oz. dried tagliatelle

1 tbsp. olive oil

1/2 onion, peeled and finely chopped

2 garlic cloves, peeled and finely chopped

1 red chili, finely chopped

100 ml./3.3 oz. white wine

30 g./2 tbsp. tomato purée

400 g./14 oz. tin pomodorino cherry tomatoes

Salt and freshly ground black pepper

NOTES FROM THE CHEF: This used to be one of my favorite meals after a heavy training session.

Bring water to a boil in a large saucepan. Season with salt. Heat the tablespoon of olive oil in a medium saucepan.

Saute the onion for two minutes, then add the chili and garlic. Pour the wine in and bring it to a boil. Cook off the wine for two minutes. Next add the tomato purée and tomatoes. Once the mixture is simmering, season with salt and pepper to taste, and continue simmering for eight to 10 minutes.

Cook the tagliatelle (similar to fettuccine) for eight to 10 minutes, or according to instructions on box. Once cooked, drain the pasta and add the sauce.

Sebastian Coe won gold medals in the 1,500m at the 1980 and 1984 Olympic Games. He set eight outdoor and three indoor world records during his career.

Fresh Pasta

Katie McGregor

I N G R E D I E N T S

Fresh pasta

Mozzarella balls

Cherry tomatoes

Vinaigrette dressing

NOTES FROM THE CHEF: My friend, Marcy Akard, introduced me to this very simple recipe on a trip to San Francisco. Since then I have fueled myself with this meal on many occasions. I also had an unbelievable version at a restaurant in Leuven, Belgium a few years ago. I love vinaigrette dressing on just about everything, so this meal is perfect for me!

Cook fresh pasta; this usually only takes a few minutes. Drain and cool the pasta, and then put into a large bowl. Cut mozzarella balls into halves or quarters, add to pasta. Cut cherry tomatoes into halves, add to pasta. Empty your desired amount of vinaigrette dressing into pasta.

Katie McGregor has won multiple USA titles on the roads, as well as the 10,000m at the 2005 USA Track & Field Championships. She frequently represents the U.S. internationally.

Artichoke Lasagna Amy Hastings

I N G R E D I E N T S

1 lb. ground beef

1 14-16 oz. can diced tomatoes

1 16 oz. can tomato sauce

1 8 oz. jar marinated artichoke hearts

4 cloves garlic, minced or pressed

8 oz. cottage cheese

3 c. mozzarella cheese, shredded

1 c. Swiss cheese, shredded

3/4 c. parmesan cheese, shredded

9 lasagna noodles

Salt to taste

Pepper to taste

Oregano to taste

Basil leaves to taste

Amy Hastings won the 2004 Pac-10 Cross Country title for Arizona State. She won the 2006 USATF National Club Cross Country Championship, and represented the U.S. at the 2008 World Cross Country Championships.

Cook the ground beef in a frying pan and drain the fat. Add the tomato sauce, diced tomatoes, garlic, salt pepper, basil leaves, and oregano. Let this simmer on medium heat for approximately 15 minutes. Stir occasionally.

In a large bowl, mix the cottage cheese, mozzarella cheese, Swiss cheese, and parmesan cheese.

Cook the lasagna noodles in boiling water for approximately 10 minutes, leaving them slightly undercooked. Drain the water.

Preheat the oven to 350°, then start assembling the lasagna in a 9x13-inch pan. First, put a light layer of the beef and tomato mixture on the bottom of the pan. Follow this with a light layer of cheese. Add a layer of three noodles, more meat and tomato, cheese, and the marinated artichoke hearts. Add another layer of noodles, then the meat mixture, cheese, the last three noodles, the remainder of the sauce, and the remainder of the cheese. Bake for 20 to 30 minutes, and let it cool before serving.

Eggplant Parmesan   Molly Huddle

INGREDIENTS

2-3 c. spaghetti sauce (I like Paul Newman's)

3-4 baby eggplants

2 eggs

2-3 c. breadcrumbs

1/4 c. olive oil

1 c. mozzarella cheese

1/4 c. parmesan cheese

NOTES FROM THE CHEF: This recipe comes from my mom, Kathy Huddle. The leftovers taste good in a sub sandwich.

Preheat oven to 350°. Start by washing and slicing the eggplants into one-quarter inch medallions. I leave the skin on, but you can peel off if you prefer.

Beat the eggs in a bowl and pour the breadcrumbs into another bowl. Dip the eggplant slices into the egg, then coat it in breadcrumbs. Sauté slices in olive oil over medium heat. Layer sautéed slices in baking dish, then pour spaghetti sauce over. Put down another eggplant layer, more sauce, and top with cheeses.

Bake for 20 to 30 minutes or until bubbly. This recipe can also include meat if desired, but I like it as is. Serve with garlic bread and salad.

Molly Huddle was a Big East champion and All-American runner for Notre Dame. She now runs professionally for Saucony and represented the U.S. at the 2008 World Cross Country Championships.

Pumpkin Lasagna Deena Kastor

I N G R E D I E N T S

1 pumpkin, peeled, seeded, and cut into 1-inch cubes (8 cups)*

5 c. lowfat milk

Fistful of sage, chopped

Big pinch of nutmeg

1 clove garlic, smashed

Fresh lasagna sheets (spinach or regular)

2 c. mozzarella cheese

2 c. parmesan cheese

Sage leaves for garnish

*You can also use butternut squash in place of the pumpkin. Just peel and cube squash.

Deena Kastor won the bronze medal in the marathon at the 2004 Olympic Games. She is also a two-time silver medalist in the 8k at the World Cross Country Championships. She holds the American record of 2:19:36 in the marathon.

Place pumpkin in stock pot with two cups of water. Cover and steam over medium heat until tender, about 15 minutes.

Preheat oven to 400°. Over medium-high heat, boil milk with chopped sage, nutmeg, and garlic. Boil for five minutes. Discard garlic and put milk mixture in blender; blend until smooth. Return to pan and simmer for 10 more minutes. Sauce can be made two days prior.

If you are not using fresh lasagna sheets, boil noodles (even no-boil variety) according to packaged instructions. In a lasagna pan, coat bottom with three tablespoons of sauce. Place a layer of noodles on top of that. On top of noodles, add one-third of pumpkin, one-third of sauce, and one-third of cheeses. Continue with another layer of noodles, followed by pumpkin, sauce, and cheese until ingredients are used.

Cover with foil, making a tent, as not to touch the top layer of cheese. Bake for 30 to 40 minutes. Uncover and bake for 10 minutes more. Let sit for five minutes before serving. Garnish individual pieces with sprigs of sage.

NOTES FROM THE CHEF: My husband Andrew and I had a pumpkin carving party a few years ago, and I made this recipe along with pumpkin soup and pumpkin green chili pie. Ryan Shay loved this lasagna, which is why I chose this as my recipe.

Mushroom Risotto   Chris Lundstrom

I N G R E D I E N T S

2 qt. cold water

1 yellow onion, peeled and thinly sliced

1 leek top, sliced and washed

8 cloves garlic in their skin, crushed with the side of a knife blade

1 tsp. salt

1 oz. dried shitake mushrooms

2 carrots, sliced

1 large unpeeled potato, sliced

2 celery ribs, sliced

1 28 oz. can crushed or whole peeled tomatoes with juice

6 parsley sprigs, coarsely chopped

6 fresh thyme sprigs

3 fresh sage leaves

2 fresh marjoram or oregano sprigs

1/2 tsp. peppercorns

To make vegetable stock, pour half a cup of the water into a stockpot. Add onion, garlic, leek top, and salt. Stir, cover, and cook over medium heat for 15 minutes.

Add the rest of the water and the remaining ingredients. Bring stock to a boil, then reduce heat and simmer uncovered for an hour.

Pour stock through a strainer, removing as much liquid as possible from the vegetables, and discard them.

Use stock immediately, or cool and refrigerate or freeze.

This is adapted from a recipe which appears in the *Field of Greens* cookbook, from the Greens Restaurant in San Francisco.

I N G R E D I E N T S

6 c. vegetable stock (from above)

1/4 oz. dried porcini mushrooms

4 tbsp. extra virgin olive oil

1-2 lb. crimini or white button mushrooms

Salt and pepper

4 cloves garlic, finely chopped

1 medium yellow onion or leek (white part only)

1-1/2 c. Arborio rice

1/2 c. dry white wine

2 tbsp. coarsely chopped Italian parsley

To make Risotto, bring half a cup of water to a boil, then remove from heat. Add dried porcini mushrooms and let soak for 10 minutes. Remove mushrooms, but save water. Finely chop porcini mushrooms.

Heat vegetable stock to boil, then leave simmering on stove.

Chop the onion. Scrub and slice crimini and/or white button mushrooms.

Heat one tablespoon of the olive oil in a large skillet. Add mushrooms, one-quarter of a teaspoon of salt, and a few pinches of pepper.

Sauté until mushrooms are golden and crisp on the edges; add half the garlic, then the porcini-soaking liquid. When most of the liquid has evaporated, transfer the mushrooms to a bowl.

(Continued on page 58)

NOTES FROM THE CHEF: This recipe is a combination of various other recipes and the process of experimentation. I like to cook risotto the night before a race. It takes some time, especially if you make your own stock, but it's really not very difficult. I find it relaxing the night before a big race. I made this before placing fourth and running a PR in the 2006 USA Marathon Championship.

Heat the remaining three tablespoons of olive oil; add the onions, along with one quarter of a teaspoon of salt, and a few pinches of pepper. Sauté over medium heat for two to three minutes, then add remaining garlic and porcini mushrooms and sauté for another one to two minutes.

Add Arborio rice, sauté for two to three minutes, stirring constantly, making sure each grain is coated with oil. Continue stirring until grains begin to lose their color slightly, but not so long that they brown.

Begin adding stock. Add half a cup at a time, stirring constantly, and making sure liquid is absorbed before adding more. After adding three cups of stock, add sautéed mushrooms and wine.

Continue slowly adding stock and stirring until rate of absorption slows markedly. The risotto should be "toothy" tender, but with a tiny bit of crispness, and the texture quite saucy. At that point, remove from heat and stir in half the parsley and additional salt and black pepper to taste. Serve and top with parsley.

Note: You must stir constantly while risotto is cooking. Failure to do so will result in poor texture. Turn some music on, grab a glass of wine, and keep on stirring—it's worth it!

Substitutions, shortcuts and embellishments:

1. Make vegetable stock using Better than Bouillon Mushroom or Vegetable Base. It's quick, easy, and better than most pre-made stocks.

2. I often use half butter and half olive oil for frying the risotto (so two tablespoons of olive oil and two tablespoons butter instead of all olive oil). The butter adds a richer flavor.

Chris Lundstrom won the 2005 Napa Valley Marathon, finished third in the 2001 USA Marathon Championships, and represented the U.S. in the marathon at the 2007 Pan American Games. Lundstrom helped Stanford win NCAA Cross Country titles in 1996 and 1997.

3. Feel free to add parmesan cheese liberally both times you add the parsley (about one-quarter of a cup each time).

Baked Spaghetti

I N G R E D I E N T S

1 c. chopped onion

1 c. chopped green pepper

1 tbsp. butter or margarine

1 can (28 oz.) tomatoes with liquid, cut up

1 can (4 oz.) mushroom stems and pieces, drained

1 can (2-1/4 oz.) sliced ripe olives, drained

2 tsp. dried oregano

1 lb. ground beef, browned and drained (optional)

12 oz. spaghetti, cooked and drained

2 c. (8 oz.) shredded cheddar cheese

1 can (10-3/4 oz.) condensed cream of mushroom soup, undiluted

1/4 c. water

1/4 c. grated parmesan cheese

Todd Williams, pictured running behind Ryan Shay in 2002, is a two-time U.S. Olympian who won four USA 10,000m titles. He recorded four top-10 Olympic and World Championships finishes during his career. Williams still holds the USA 15k record.

Preheat oven to 350°. In a large skillet, sauté onion and green pepper in butter until tender. Add the tomatoes, mushrooms, olives, and oregano. Add ground beef, if desired. Simmer uncovered for 10 minutes.

Place half of the cooked and drained spaghetti in a greased 13x9-inch baking dish. Top with half of the vegetable mixture. Sprinkle with one cup of cheddar cheese. Repeat layers in order. Mix the soup and water until smooth, then pour over the casserole. Sprinkle with parmesan cheese. Bake uncovered for 30-35 minutes or until heated through. Makes 12 servings.

NOTES FROM THE CHEF: My mother made this for me back in high school, before my meets. I was convinced it made me run faster! Enjoy this "magic" recipe.

Penne Giardiniera

Kathy Butler

I N G R E D I E N T S

2 bundles of spinach
Butter
1-1/2 tbsp. chili powder
2/3 tbsp. nutmeg
1 egg
2 c. grated Grano Padano or any mild grateable cheese
4 cloves crushed garlic
2 cloves garlic
1 c. breadcrumbs, plus a few more for rolling
Vegetable oil for frying balls
4 medium zucchini
2 tsp. chili powder
Penne or another type of pasta for four

NOTES FROM THE CHEF: This tasty pasta has been a favorite at our house. Elva Dryer, Nicole Aish, Mike Aish, Mara Yamauchi, Shige Yamauchi, Andrew Leatherby, Meg Leatherby, Stephanie Bylander, and Matt Levasieur are just a few from the running community who have enjoyed it.

Remove stems from spinach and wash leaves. Steam spinach for three minutes. Pour cold water over spinach. Squeeze spinach into a big ball, squeezing as much water out as possible. Tear spinach into little pieces, ripping the leaves apart. Do not use a knife. Place in a large bowl.

Add bread crumbs, egg, garlic, chili powder, nutmeg, and cheese to large bowl with spinach. Mix well.

Form one ball, with a roughly one-inch diameter, from the mixture. Roll ball in breadcrumbs. Fry one ball in vegetable oil until breadcrumbs turn a golden color. Taste and add more chili powder, nutmeg, or garlic if necessary.

Form the rest of the mixture into balls. While cooking pasta, start to fry these balls. Cook enough pasta for four. It doesn't have to be penne.

Grate zucchini into big, long strips. In pan, sweat zucchini, garlic, and chili powder in butter. To serve, toss zucchini with pasta and put spinach balls on top.

Serves four. When prepared as above, this is vegetarian, but it is good with sliced grilled chicken as well.

Kathy Butler is a 2004 British Olympian at 10,000m. She won four NCAA titles for the University of Wisconsin, and also won the 2004 and 2005 British 10,000m title.

Stuffed Pasta Shells

Josh Rohatinsky

I N G R E D I E N T S

18 (6 oz.) jumbo pasta shells

2 tbsp. melted margarine

1-1/4 lb. ground beef

3 oz. cream cheese

1-2 tsp. chili powder (depending on preference)

1/4 tsp. salt

1 c. mild salsa

1 c. cheddar cheese

1 c. mozzarella

1-1/2 c. crushed tortilla chips

Cook the pasta shells according to the instructions on the box. Drain pasta and toss with melted margarine. Preheat oven to 350°.

Brown the ground beef and drain the grease. Stir cream cheese, chili powder, and salt into browned beef, and cook until the cream cheese is melted.

Fill the pasta shells with the meat mixture and put onto greased 9x13-inch pan. Spoon salsa on top of the shells, then cover them with foil.

Bake for 15 minutes, then take foil off and add cheese and chips to the top. Bake for another 10 to 15 minutes uncovered. Sprinkle with parsley and serve.

NOTES FROM THE CHEF: This recipe comes from my wife's cousin, Christy Smith. I love pasta, but I also just cannot go without lots of meat! So this Italian-Mexican cross recipe is a really good combo.

Josh Rohatinsky won the 2006 NCAA Cross Country title for BYU. In his debut marathon, he finished ninth in the 2008 Olympic Marathon Trials in 2:15:22.

Stuffed Acorn Squash   Michael and Kristi Spence

I N G R E D I E N T S

1 acorn squash

Olive oil

Salt and pepper

1 clove garlic, minced

1/2 lb. small pasta or other small grain*

2 chicken sausages (or 1 chicken breast), cut into small pieces**

2-3 tbsp. fresh pesto

3-4 tomatoes, chopped

2-3 slices fresh mozzarella cheese, cut into small pieces

*Orzo will work well, as will heartier grains like barley or wheatberries. Trader Joe's (if you have one near you) makes a really great harvest grain blend that is perfect. You can also make risotto and stuff the squash with risotto.

**We really like the Han's All Natural Brand—the sausage comes fully cooked, and several varieties of gourmet flavors are available. Chicken or more traditional sausage will work just as well.

Michael Spence represented the U.S. at the 2007 World Cross Country Championships and won a silver medal in the 3,000m steeplechase at the 2007 Pan American Games. Kristi Spence is a 2:45 marathoner and Olympic Trials qualifier.

P reheat oven to 350°. Cut the acorn squash in half; scoop out and discard the seeds. Drizzle each half with olive oil, and sprinkle with salt and pepper. Place, cut-side down, on a baking sheet and roast for one hour.

Cook pasta to desired tenderness. In a separate sauté pan, while the pasta is cooking and the squash is continuing to roast, heat one teaspoon of olive oil. Add garlic and stir to avoid burning. Cook for about one minute. Add sausage or chicken and cook until done. Add tomatoes and continue to cook for about two additional minutes.

Add sausage mixture to pasta and stir in pesto. When done, remove squash from oven and spoon pasta into the center of each squash half. Top with diced fresh mozzarella cheese and enjoy!

NOTES FROM THE CHEF: We originally found a Southwestern-style version of this recipe in *Eating Well* magazine, but have since adapted it to the more Italian-style flavors that we prefer. This recipe is very flexible, and stuffing the squash is a fun way to serve a pasta dish. It is perfect for runners, because it has plenty of nutrient-dense carbohydrates.

Mokimo

I N G R E D I E N T S

10-12 potatoes (2 to 3 potatoes per person, depending on the size), peeled and cut up

2 lb. dried corn and dried beans or peas (any type, such as kidney)

1 bag of baby spinach (or any type of greens)

Salt to taste

1 large red or white onion, chopped

2-3 tsp. vegetable oil

3 c. water

Sauté the onion in oil until it is golden brown. Add potatoes to the onion and let them cook for three to five minutes, to brown. Then add water and some salt, bring to a boil, and let the potatoes soften.

When they have softened but are not too soft yet, add the corn and bean mixture (called githeri) and the spinach, then cover and let cook. When the spinach is well-cooked and the potatoes are soft, remove pot from heat. Drain the water and save it.

With a potato masher, mash the mixture together, gradually adding the reserved water to moisten. Mixture should be firm like stiff mashed potatoes, not runny and not hard. Check seasoning and add more salt if needed. This can be served alone or with some chicken or beef stew. Serves four.

NOTES FROM THE CHEF: This is a typical Kikuyu dish, and it's my husband's favorite.

Catherine Ndereba won the marathon at the 2003 and 2007 World Championships. She won a silver medal in the marathon at the 2004 Olympic Games, and silver in the marathon at the 2005 World Championships. Ndereba is a former world record holder in the marathon, with a PR of 2:18:47.

Chicken Pilaf

Hendrick Ramaala

I N G R E D I E N T S

10 ml./2 tsp. oil or oil spray

1 medium onion, chopped

1 clove of garlic, chopped

2 medium carrots, cut into julienne strips

1 green pepper, cut into strips

500 ml./2 c. rice, cooked

500 ml./2 c. chicken, cooked and chopped (about 4-6 pieces/450 g. skinless breast/ thighs)

125 ml./1/2 c. chicken stock

15 ml./1 tbsp. soy sauce

50 ml./3 tbsp. white wine or chicken stock

1 slice feta cheese, crumbled (optional)

Preparation time: approximately 20 minutes
Cooking time: approximately 15 minutes

Sauté the onion and garlic in a pan with the oil or oil spray, until they become translucent. Add the carrot strips and continue sautéing for an additional minute. Add the green pepper, and sauté until it is soft, but still firm. Add the rice.

In a separate container, mix the chicken, soy sauce, and white wine or chicken stock. Once mixed, add to the rice and vegetable mixture and heat through.

Mix in the feta cheese gently and serve.

This is adapted from a recipe in *High Performance Winning Recipes*, published by the South African Sports Commission.

Hendrick Ramaala is the 2004 ING New York City Marathon champion. He won silver medals at the World Half Marathon Championships in 1998 and 1999.

> NOTES FROM THE CHEF: This is the meal I go for after those heavy and demanding long, long runs.

Lemon Rosemary Chicken — Jen Toomey

INGREDIENTS

3 lb. chicken*

2+ cloves garlic, minced

2 lemons, cut into quarters

2 tbsp. capers

2 tbsp. rosemary

1/2 c. black olives (optional, the ones marinated in olive oil are best)

*Thighs are the easiest, but if you want a lowfat version, soak chicken breasts with bone in a saltwater brine for two-plus hours. To make a saltwater brine, put about one cup of salt into a pot of cold water. This makes the chicken very tender.

Heat a large skillet (cast iron is key for this). Add capers. Cook capers until there is very little liquid left. The skillet will look white from this.

Add chicken and brown on both sides. Add lemon, rosemary, black olives, and garlic. Put entire pan into oven at 350° for 30 minutes, or until chicken is cooked through. Add liquid such as water, white wine, or chicken broth if chicken seems dry in cooking process.

This is perfect over rice, pasta, or my favorite, quinoa.

NOTES FROM THE CHEF: This is my favorite dish. I first started making it a couple of years ago after having something similar in a small café in London after running in the Crystal Palace. It's easy to make and has some very powerful ingredients that help the body recover. Lemons and capers are strong alkalinizing agents (very good for neutralizing lactic acid). Garlic boosts the immune system, and rosemary has been used for centuries to boost circulation.

Jen Toomey is the 2004 and 2005 USA Indoor 1,500m champion, as well as the 2004 USA Indoor 800m champion. She set the American indoor record for 1,000m in 2004, and finished fourth in the 800m at the 2004 World Indoor Track & Field Championships.

Chicken Tetrazzini

Melissa Cook

I N G R E D I E N T S

7 oz. spaghetti, broken into thirds

1/4 c. butter or margarine

1/4 c. all-purpose flour

1/2 tsp. salt

1/4 tsp. pepper

1 c. chicken broth

1 c. heavy whipping cream

2 tbsp. dry sherry

2 c. cubed cooked chicken

4.5 oz. jar sliced mushrooms, drained

1/2 c. grated parmesan cheese

Preparation time: 20 minutes
Cooking time: 30 minutes

Preheat oven to 350°. Cook the spaghetti according to the instructions on the package. Drain.

While cooking spaghetti, melt butter over low heat in a two-quart saucepan. Stir in the flour, salt, and pepper. Continue to cook, stirring constantly, until the mixture is smooth and bubbly.

Remove saucepan from heat, and stir in the broth and whipping cream. Return saucepan to heat, and heat until boiling. Let mixture boil for one minute while stirring constantly.

Stir the spaghetti, sherry, chicken, and mushrooms into the sauce. Pour contents of saucepan into an ungreased two-quart casserole. Sprinkle top with parmesan cheese.

Bake uncovered for about 30 minutes, or until it's bubbly in the center. Makes six servings.

Melissa Cook finished sixth in the 10,000m at the 2004 U.S. Olympic Trials. She was a multi-time NCAA runner-up and All-American for Texas A&M.

Garden Chicken Mandi Zemba

I N G R E D I E N T S

4 thawed boneless, skinless chicken breasts

1 tbsp. Italian seasoning

8 oz. organic soybean pods

8 oz. frozen mixed vegetables

2 tbsp. grapeseed oil

1/2 c. slivered almonds

Whole grain brown rice (optional)

Cut chicken breasts into half-inch slices. Heat an electric skillet on medium heat and add grapeseed oil. Add chicken and Italian seasoning. Sauté chicken for two minutes.

Add mixed vegetables, soybean pods, and almonds; cover for six minutes. Stir occasionally until chicken has reached an internal temperature of 165°. Serve over whole grain brown rice, if desired, and enjoy!

> NOTES FROM THE CHEF: This recipe was designed by my husband, Brian Zemba, based on my needs and requests. He is the cook in the family. I like to eat this meal after a hard workout to get in some protein and replenish some good vitamins to help me recover better.

Mandi Zemba was an eight-time NCAA DII champion for Grand Valley State University. She now runs professionally for New Balance and has represented the U.S. internationally.

Salmon Fillets Steamed in Orange and Honey Mary Cullen

I N G R E D I E N T S

4 fresh organic salmon fillet steaks

1/2 c. freshly squeezed orange juice with zest

1/2 c. blossom honey (or similarly fragrant honey)

Sea salt and black pepper to taste

Preheat oven to 400°. Wash and dry the salmon fillets. Place each in a square of aluminum foil, season well with salt and pepper, and drizzle the orange juice and honey mixture on top. Wrap up the foil and place in the oven for 15 to 20 minutes, until just cooked through.

Mary Cullen, a native of Ireland, won the 2006 NCAA 5,000m title for Providence College. She now runs professionally for Reebok.

Meat, Roasted Potatoes, Asparagus, and Salad   Alistair Cragg

I N G R E D I E N T S

I N G R E D I E N T S

Olive oil

Fresh rosemary

Salt and pepper

Red potatoes

Yellow onions

Garlic

To make the rosemary roasted potatoes, preheat oven to 400°. Mix together the olive oil, fresh rosemary, salt, pepper, red potatoes, yellow onions, and garlic. In order for the onions to not burn, cook the potatoes for 15 to 20 minutes before adding the onions. Cook in oven for 45 minutes to an hour, or until golden brown. If you have a convection oven use that; it makes them crispier.

Alistair Cragg is an Irish Olympian who won seven NCAA titles while at the University of Arkansas. He won the 3,000m at the 2005 European Indoor Championships, and he holds Irish records at 3,000m, 5,000m, and 10,000m.

I N G R E D I E N T S

Olive oil

Salt and pepper

Asparagus

Parmesan cheese

To make the asparagus, preheat oven to 375°. Place asparagus on a cookie sheet. Sprinkle a small amount of olive oil on the asparagus, along with salt and pepper. Roast asparagus for 10 to 20 minutes. Sprinkle with parmesan cheese immediately after removing from oven.

I N G R E D I E N T S

Baby arugula lettuce

Tomato

Avocado

Red onion

Olive oil

Balsamic vinegar

Salt and pepper

Mix all ingredients using proportions of your choosing.

NOTES FROM THE CHEF: This is a balanced meal but it tastes delicious, which, as we know in most cases, isn't that healthy for you. After my last hard workout of the week, my girlfriend and I go to the local market and pick up some fresh meat, which varies depending on what I crave or what my body needs. The greatest cook I know whips together this great meal while I lounge and stretch in front of the TV. She told me her secret is that she always uses Wishbone Italian to marinade any meet she grills. It's good on fish, steaks, and chicken. She also uses it for the vegetable kabobs. This is obviously far more work than I'd go through for most meals, but it certainly serves as a treat at the end of a hard week of running.

Salmon with Salad

I N G R E D I E N T S

Any kind of fresh salmon with skin (wild is preferable), 1/4 lb. per person.

1/4 lb. fresh mixed greens per person

1/4 lb. sweet potatoes per person

1/4 lb. mushrooms

4 cloves garlic

1 shallot (any onion is a fine substitute).

Bell peppers (optional)

Jalapeño peppers (optional)

Chives, carrots, tomatoes, etc. (any other veggies you like on your salad)

Grapeseed oil (canola oil is fine)

Olive oil (for salad)

Black pepper, finely ground

Sea salt

2 lemons or limes

Balsamic vinegar (any vinegar, lemon, lime, and oranges are fine substitutes)

Tools:
- Cast-iron skillet
- Oven or outside grill
- Small frying pan (for sautéing mushrooms)
- Small pot (for boiling sweet potatoes)
- Large salad bowl
- Small bowl (for marinating salmon)

Bolota Asmerom was a 2000 Eritrean Olympian at 5,000m, and is now a U.S. citizen. He finished third in the 5,000m at the 2004 U.S. Olympic Trials, and was an All-American distance runner for the University of California-Berkeley.

To marinate the salmon, cut it into eight- to 10-ounce pieces, wash, and place in mixing bowl. Add the juice of one to two lemons or limes, two cloves of garlic (crushed or diced), desired amount of sea salt and ground black pepper, four tablespoons of grapeseed oil. Mix, and then refrigerate for 30 minutes or more.

Sweet Potato-Mixed Greens Salad: Chop half of the shallots or onions into thin, long pieces. Slice tomatoes. Dice one clove of garlic. Place above ingredients in a salad bowl and mix with desired amounts of olive oil, balsamic vinegar, sea salt, and black pepper. Let this marinate while the salmon cooks and the sweet potatoes boil. Add the rest of the ingredients when the salmon is ready. Blueberries, walnuts, and raisins always add interesting texture

Mushrooms: Slice a desired amount of mushrooms, the remainder of the shallots or onions, and dice one clove of garlic. Sauté above ingredients with grapeseed oil in a small frying pan. Mix mushrooms with the salad, or place them on top of the salmon.

Sweet potatoes: Wash but do not peel sweet potatoes, and chop them into one-inch pieces. Boil potatoes in water, without over-boiling. Strain potatoes and let them cool to room temperature before mixing them with the salad.

Salmon: Prepare the salmon last to preserve its heat and flavor. Preheat the oven to 350° to 400°. Sear the salmon, with skin on the bottom, in a pan for three to four minutes. Place the salmon in the oven for five additional minutes. The acid in the lemon will have tenderized the salmon, therefore you won't need much heat. Place the salmon on top of the salad. The skin will easily peel off if you prefer it that way. Skip all of the steps above and simply grill the salmon to your preference if you are using an outdoor grill.

Ground Beef Turnovers

Lindsey Anderson

INGREDIENTS

4 c. all-purpose flour
1 tbsp. sugar
2 tsp. salt
1-3/4 c. shortening
1/2 c. ice water
1 egg, lightly beaten
1 tbsp. vinegar
2 lb. uncooked lean ground beef
1 c. diced carrots
2 medium potatoes, peeled and cut into 1/4-inch cubes
1 medium onion, chopped
1-2 tsp. salt
1/4 tsp. pepper
Half-and-half cream

As a senior at Weber State University in 2007, Lindsey Anderson set a collegiate record of 9:39.95 in the 3,000m steeplechase.

Combine the flour, sugar, and salt in a mixing bowl. Gradually add in the shortening, until mixture resembles coarse crumbs. In a separate bowl, combine the water, egg, and vinegar, mixing well. Add to shortening mixture, one tablespoon at a time. Lightly toss the mixture until it forms a ball. Cover bowl and chill for 30 minutes.

Preheat oven to 375°. To make the filling, combine the ground beef, carrots, potatoes, onion, salt, and pepper. Once the pastry has chilled for 30 minutes, divide it into 15 equal portions. Roll out one portion on a surface lightly sprinkled with flour. It should be a circle with a six- to seven-inch diameter.

Place a heaping one-third cup of filling on half of the circle. Moisten the edges with water, then fold the dough over, pressing the edges with a fork to seal. Transfer the turnover to a greased baking sheet. Repeat this with the remaining pastry and filling.

Cut three slits in the top of each turnover, then brush with cream. Bake for 35-40 minutes, or until the vegetables are tender and the pastry crust is golden brown. Makes 15 turnovers.

This is adapted from a recipe which originally appeared in *Country Woman* magazine.

NOTES FROM THE CHEF: My husband and I love these! This recipe is a little time consuming, but the extras keep well in the refrigerator, and you could even freeze them for longer if needed. Hope you all enjoy!

Side Dishes,
Appetizers,
Beverages,
&
Snacks

Meatballs
Patti Dillon

I N G R E D I E N T S

1 lb. ground chuck

4 oz. dried breadcrumbs

4 large eggs

4 oz. whole milk

6 oz. grated romano cheese

3 oz. grated Spanish onion

2 oz. fresh garlic, finely diced

2 oz. fresh Italian parsley leaves, finely chopped

2 oz. fresh basil leaves, finely chopped

Preheat oven to 350°, and spray a baking sheet with olive oil cooking spray. In a large bowl, mix all of the ingredients well. Add additional breadcrumbs if the mixture does not seem thick enough.

Roll mixture into meatballs which are approximately the size of golf balls. Place meatballs on a baking sheet and cook them for approximately 35 to 40 minutes.

Here's an easy, great-tasting sauce to put on your meatballs:

I N G R E D I E N T S

6 oz. good olive oil, not extra-virgin

12 cloves garlic, finely sliced

1 large or 2 medium Spanish onions, finely diced

1 large handful julienned fresh basil leaves

2 28-oz. cans imported crushed tomatoes

1 tsp. salt

1/2 tsp. white or black pepper

Put oil in a medium saucepan, and cook over medium heat. Once oil is heated, add the garlic and onions to the pan. Continue cooking over medium heat until they're soft and slightly brown.

Add the crushed tomatoes, salt, and pepper. Stir. Once the sauce comes to a simmer, cook for 20 minutes. Remove sauce from heat and add the julienned basil.

Patti Dillon was the first American woman to break 2:30 in the marathon. She once held world bests for 5 miles, 10k, 20k, the half marathon, and 30k. She has been inducted into the National Distance Running Hall of Fame.

Bean and Avocado Potato
Mary Cullen

I N G R E D I E N T S

4 large evenly shaped potatoes - about 300 g. each

290 g./10 oz. red kidney beans

200 g./7 oz. jar taco sauce (e.g. Old El Paso)

1/2 avocado

2 tbsp. fresh coriander or parsley

Preheat oven to 415°. Wash the potatoes and pat them dry with a paper towel. Puncture the potatoes several times with a small, sharp knife. Place potatoes directly on oven rack. Bake for at least one hour. If you prefer really crip skins, leave potatoes in oven for 90 minutes.

Rinse and drain the kidney beans, then place them in a small saucepan with the taco sauce. Place saucepan over medium heat, until mixture is warmed through.

Once potatoes are done cooking, cut them in half and scoop their flesh into a bowl. Mash the insides of the potatoes with the avocado, then return the mixture to the potato skins. Spoon the bean mixture over the top. Serve with coriander or parsley on top.

Mary Cullen, a native of Ireland, won the 2006 NCAA 5,000m title for Providence College. She now runs professionally for Reebok.

Cream Cheese Mashed Potatoes   Nikeya Green

I N G R E D I E N T S

3 lb. peeled potatoes

1/2 to 3/4 c. milk

1 3 oz. package of cream cheese, softened

Salt and pepper to taste

Boil the potatoes in a large pot, until they are tender. Drain potatoes. Mash potatoes until they are smooth, the beat in the milk, cream cheese, butter, salt, and pepper. Continue beating until the potatoes are light and fluffy.

Nikeya Green, an All-American runner while at Wake Forest University, won the 800m title at the 2006 USA Indoor Track & Field Championships.

NOTES FROM THE CHEF: I have always been a huge fan of potatoes! I love potato chips, baked potatoes, and I especially love mashed potatoes. This is one of my favorite kinds of mashed potatoes. I first had it at dinner at a friend's house. I would have to say that it is one of the most delicious things that has ever hit my taste buds. Both of my parents are from the south, so I grew up on southern style meals. This recipe makes me feel right at home. Plus, it is so simple to make and absolutely delicious! Hope you enjoy!

Cornflake Potatoes   Mark and Kelly Conover

I N G R E D I E N T S

32 oz. cubed frozen hash browns

2 c. sour cream

1 small chopped onion

1 can cream of chicken soup

1 stick of melted butter

2 c. grated cheese

Crushed cornflakes

Defrost hashbrowns. Preheat oven to 350°. Mix sour cream, soup, onion, and butter with the defrosted hash browns. Then stir in the cheese.

Spread mixture evenly into a 9x13-inch pan. Crush cornflakes over the top. Bake for 45 to 60 minutes.

NOTES FROM THE CHEF: This is a recipe everyone likes. Kelly got this recipe from Kristin Timm, formerly Wellman, another ASU running alum. This dish is perfect for replenishing the body after a workout. Taste buds, caloric intake, carbs, and glycogen stores will all be satisfied with this dish. This recipe is great for potlucks, barbecues, and even as an extra component of a big breakfast. You can also add cubed ham and make it a meal by itself.

Kelly (Cordell) Conover was an All-American distance runner for Arizona State University, and has qualified for the Olympic Trials in the 10,000m and marathon. Mark Conover became a 1988 U.S. Olympian by winning the 1988 U.S. Olympic Marathon Trials.

Red Onion Potato Gratin   Peter Gilmore

I N G R E D I E N T S

4-5 large (6-7 medium) Yukon gold potatoes

1 large red onion

2 sprigs of fresh thyme or rosemary

1 c. olive oil

2 tbsp. butter

Salt and pepper

Preheat oven to 425°. Slice the onion by first cutting in half, and then cutting into very thin slices. Place in frying pan with two tablespoons of olive oil and the thyme or rosemary sprigs. Cover and cook on low heat for 10 to 12 minutes, or until the onion has softened and absorbed the thyme or rosemary flavor.

While the onion is cooking, slice the potatoes into thin, round slices. Place the slices in a large bowl of water. To wash the excess starch off the potato slices, change the water several times while you slice the remaining potatoes.

Pour the water out of the bowl and use a clean towel to dry the water off of the potato slices. By this point, the onion should have softened.

Line a heavy bottomed casserole dish with olive oil. Place a layer of the dry potato slices in the bottom of the pan. They should overlap slightly, almost like fish scales. Add about one-third of the onions on top of the first layer of potatoes, along with some salt and pepper. Continue adding alternating layers of potato and onion (with salt and pepper), making sure the top layer is made up of potato slices. Place small knobs of butter around the top of the dish, along with some salt and pepper. Drizzle about three-quarters of a cup of olive oil all over the top of the dish.

Bake in 425° oven for about 50 minutes, or until the top is golden brown.

Peter Gilmore finished seventh in the 2006 Boston Marathon in a PR 2:12:45, and eighth in the 2008 U.S. Olympic Marathon Trials.

NOTES FROM THE CHEF: This potato gratin is a little different because it relies on olive oil, instead of cheese or cream, for richness. It's also a good example of how a few simple ingredients, combined with good kitchen techniques, can yield something unexpectedly delicious.

Candied Yams

Khadevis Robinson

I N G R E D I E N T S

Yams or sweet potatoes

Karo Syrup (light or dark)

Granulated sugar

Butter or margarine

Vanilla

Nutmeg

Peel yams or sweet potatoes. Cut them lengthways and crossways. This should result in four pieces.

Boil the potatoes over medium heat, until that magical moment when they are no longer hard but not yet soft. Pour off the water.

Add Karo Syrup, sugar, butter, vanilla, and nutmeg to taste. Boil on low heat until the potatoes have reached desired softness.

My wife usually buys three potatoes, and she thinks, based on eyeballing it, the quantities would rougly be:

6 tbsp. Karo Syrup
1/2 c. granulated sugar
1/2 stick butter or margarine
1 tsp. vanilla
1 tbsp. nutmeg

Khadevis Robinson is the 1999, 2005, 2006, and 2007 USA Outdoor 800m champion, as well as the 1999, 2006, and 2008 USA Indoor 800m champion. He won the 1998 NCAA Outdoor 800m title for Texas Christian University.

NOTES FROM THE CHEF: This is one of my wife's favorite side dishes to cook. I submitted it because she loves to cook it and thus I love to eat it. She tries to say it is a sweet vegetable dish but once you try it, I know you will agree with me and consider it a dessert. Sorry there are no exact measurements, but believe it or not, this is the way it's been passed though the family. The recipe is meant to have a rich flavor, so I hope you have a sweet tooth.

Chrissey's Summer Corn Salad — Pete and Chrissey Pfitzinger

INGREDIENTS

4 cobs fresh sweet corn

6 medium vine-ripe tomatoes, cut into small chunks

1 small red onion, chopped

1-1/2 tbsp. white wine vinegar

1/4 c. fresh chopped coriander

1/4 tsp. salt

Fresh ground black pepper to taste

1/4 c. extra virgin olive oil

1 avocado

1/4 c. fresh grated parmesan cheese

Cook the corn, remove from the cob, and put in large bowl. Add the chopped tomatoes and onions.

Mix together white wine vinegar, olive oil, coriander, salt, and black pepper and add to the bowl. When you are close to serving this, add cut-up avocado and top with freshly grated parmesan cheese.

NOTES FROM THE CHEF: This recipe originally came from the newspaper, but it has evolved big-time over the years to reach the current state of perfection. This is the perfect salad for summer barbecues.

Pete Pfitzinger is a two-time U.S. Olympian in the marathon. He finished 11th in the 1984 Olympic Marathon and 14th in the 1988 Olympic Marathon. Chrissey Pfitzinger is a 1988 New Zealand Olympian in the 3,000m.

Portabella Sesquepedeliana — Gerry Lindgren

INGREDIENTS

4-8 large portabella mushrooms

3 tbsp. olive oil or vegetable oil

Black pepper to taste

Soy sauce to taste

Take four to eight large portabella mushrooms and cut them into bite-sized pieces. Put three tablespoons of oil (olive oil is best if you have it, but any vegetable oil is fine) in a frying pan, and put the mushrooms in to fry.

Stir often to assure they are cooking on both sides evenly. After about five minutes, turn off the heat and add black pepper and soy sauce generously. I put a toothpick through each piece to make it easier to pick up.

NOTES FROM THE CHEF: Usually when I need to prepare something for a potluck party, this is what I make.

Gerry Lindgren still holds the U.S. indoor high school record for two miles, which he set in 1964. He held the outdoor high school 5,000m record for 40 years. Lindgren was an 11-time NCAA champion for Washington State and a 1964 U.S. Olympian at 10,000m.

Guacamole

Amy Mortimer

I N G R E D I E N T S

2 ripe avocados

1/2 vine ripened tomato

2 tbsp. lemon juice

1-1/2 tsp. garlic salt

1/4 white onion chopped

Scoop avocado out of skin, place in bowl, and mash with a fork. Sprinkle lemon juice over the mashed avocado. Mix in chopped tomato, garlic salt, and onion. Let sit half an hour after mixing.

NOTES FROM THE CHEF: I learned this recipe from my dad, Bob Mortimer, and like to eat it after workouts.

Amy Mortimer was a 12-time NCAA All-American for Kansas State University. She finished third in the 1,500m at the 2005 USA Outdoor Track & Field Championships and was a member of a bronze medal winning team at the 2005 World Cross Country Championships.

Fast Smoked Salmon Canape

Kathrine Switzer

I N G R E D I E N T S

Nice brown bread, crusts off, cut into 2-inch squares, or any kind of cracker

Package of smoked salmon pieces

Small carton of sour cream or crème fraîche

Small jar of black caviar

Parsley or something green for plate decoration

Put a piece of the salmon on the bread or the cracker, and put a dollop of sour cream on top of that. Next add a very small spoonful of caviar on top of that.

Arrange on a plate and decorate with parsley. It's superb with champagne to kick off the party.

NOTES FROM THE CHEF: For dinner parties, I am always in a rush and never have time to fix anything that looks fabulous to serve with cocktails. This is really fast and can be passed around.

Kathrine Switzer is the first woman to officially run the Boston Marathon, as well as the 1974 New York City Marathon champion.

Grandma D's Apple Butter

Matt Gabrielson

I N G R E D I E N T S

6-10 apples*
1-3/4 c. sugar
1 tsp. ground cinnamon
1/4 tsp. ground cloves
2 dashes nutmeg

*Winesap, Jonathan, and Braeburn are all good. I use whatever is given to me in the apple season—some cook better than others.

Preheat oven to 350°. Quarter apples, leaving skins and core on. Cook, stirring often, with small amount of water, until tender. Add more water if needed. Push through a colander to get pulp. Discard the skins and cores. (I guess if you peel and core the apples before cooking them, you could use a blender afterwards to get the pulp.) Keep the pulp as thick as possible.

Put four cups of pulp (or as much as you are making) into a large roaster pan. To each four cups of apple pulp, add quantities of sugar, ground cinnamon, ground cloves, and nutmeg listed above. Stir well. Bake uncovered for two to three hours. Stir well at intervals. Cook until applesauce has reached the desired thickness.

Fill jars to three-quarters of an inch from the top. Refrigerate overnight and then freeze.

NOTES FROM THE CHEF: I always put this apple butter on a piece of toast in the morning before a run or an early morning race. It is so, so good. Like my other recipe, it's from Grandma Doris Gabrielson. I usually double or triple the recipe, because I get pails full of apples.

Matt Gabrielson has represented the U.S. at the World Cross Country Championships three times. He finished second at the 2005 USA Half Marathon Championships.

Spiced Hot Dark Chocolate

Kassi Andersen

INGREDIENTS

1 qt. soy milk

6 oz. dark chocolate, coarsely chopped

1/2 tsp. ground cinnamon

1/8 to 1/4 tsp. ground cardamom

1/8 tsp. ground cayenne pepper

1/8 tsp. coarse salt

Combine all of the ingredients in a small saucepan, and warm over medium-low heat while stirring. Heat for approximately five minutes, until the chocolate is completely melted and the beverage is steaming hot. Makes four servings.

This is adapted from a recipe which originally appeared at marthastewart.com.

Kassi Andersen won the 2003 NCAA 3,000m steeplechase title for Brigham Young University. She finished second in the steeplechase at the 2003 and 2004 USA Track & Field Championships.

NOTES FROM THE CHEF: This is a hot drink that runners can enjoy in the winter and cold weather. It is made with dark chocolate with spices added, so it has great flavor and some health benefits! I enjoy a cup after a workout while I ice my legs!

Mrs. Jackson's Famous Natural Energy Bars   Victoria Jackson

I N G R E D I E N T S

3/4 c. firmly packed light brown sugar

1/2 c. granulated sugar

8 oz. container vanilla or fruit-flavored lowfat yogurt

2 egg whites, lightly beaten

2 tbsp. vegetable oil (possible to substitute with applesauce)

2 tbsp. skim milk

2 tsp. vanilla extract

1-1/2 c. all-purpose flour

1 tsp. baking soda

1 tsp. ground cinnamon

1/2 tsp. salt

3 c. uncooked oats (either quick or old-fashioned)

1 c. diced dried mixed fruit, raisins, or cranberries

1/2 c. mixed nuts

2 tbsp. flaxseed (optional)

1 tsp. ground ginger (optional)

Victoria Jackson was the 2006 NCAA 10,000m champion for Arizona State. She now runs professionally for Nike.

Preheat oven to 350°. In a large bowl, combine both sugars, yogurt, beaten egg whites, oil/applesauce, milk, and vanilla extract; mix well.

In a medium bowl, combine flour, baking soda, cinnamon, salt, flaxseed (optional), and ginger (optional); mix well. Add the dry ingredients to the yogurt mixture in the large bowl; mix well.

Stir in oats, dried fruit, and mixed nuts (optional). Spread the dough onto the bottom of an ungreased 13x9-inch baking pan. Bake for 25 to 32 minutes, or until bars are light brown and a knife placed in the middle comes out clean. Remove from oven and cool completely on a wire rack. Cut into bars; makes two dozen. Power up for fast races, or enjoy as a post-workout recovery treat!

NOTES FROM THE CHEF: These bars are a great way to make friends throughout the running community. My mom, Amy Jackson, started making these natural energy bars when I was competing in high school cross country and track & field in Illinois. My mom is one of those people who knows everybody and everyone is drawn to her energetic and outgoing personality. She began to bring huge batches of the bars to high school invitationals and big meets. Friends and competitors from other Illinois high schools fell in love with my mom's bars (and my bubbly mom). Many of these Illinois kids went on to run collegiately and even professionally, and my mom still makes her energy bars to bring to races and events. Now I make them to share with training partners and friends.

Desserts

Magic Cookie Bars   Jenny Crain

INGREDIENTS

1/2 c. butter

l-1/2 c. graham cracker crumbs

14 oz. condensed milk

6 oz. bag of chocolate chips

3-1/2 oz. bag of coconut

Preheat oven to 350°. Melt the butter, then stir in the crumbs. Place the mixture in the bottom of a pan. Pour the milk over the crumbs. Top with chocolate chips and coconut. Bake for 25 minutes.

NOTES ON THIS RECIPE: This recipe was submitted by Donna Crain, her mother, on Jenny's behalf. Crain says, "Jenny loved to make magic cookie bars. They're not very healthy, but she loved them."

Jenny Crain was the top U.S. finisher (15th) at the 2004 ING New York City Marathon.

Raven's Chocolate Chip Cookies   Patti Dillon

INGREDIENTS

1/4 c. Crisco

8 tbsp. unsalted butter, soft but still firm

1 c. packed light brown sugar

1/2 c. granulated sugar

1 large egg

1 large egg white

2 tsp. vanilla extract

2 c. all-purpose flour

1/4 tsp. baking powder

1/8 tsp. salt

10 oz. chocolate (I like to use the chunks)

1-1/2 c. walnuts or pecans (optional)

Preheat oven to 375°. Beat the Crisco and butter together until smooth. Add both sugars and stir until well blended. Add egg, egg white, and vanilla, and beat until smooth.

In a separate bowl, mix flour, baking powder, and salt. Add to the batter and mix together until smooth. Add the chips (what you may have left—I eat them so I have to work fast!).

Scoop out a ball and place on cookie sheet lined with parchment paper. Bake for about 12 minutes. Eat hot, warm (best served with chilled milk), or cool. Enjoy!

NOTES FROM THE CHEF: Shhh! They're the best! These cookies are a three-time blue ribbon winner at the county fair! One of the things the Dillons do together (other than run every day) is watch *Throwdown! With Bobby Flay* on the Food Network.

Patti Dillon was the first American woman to break 2:30 in the marathon. She once held world bests for 5 miles, 10k, 20k, the half marathon, and 30k.

82

INGREDIENTS

Vanilla wafers

3/4 c. freshly-squeezed, strained lemon juice

1 can Eagle Brand condensed milk

Whipping cream

Crush up enough vanilla wafers to cover the bottom of a flat-bottom bowl. (I use one that is about six by nine inches and two to three inches deep.)

In a mixing bowl, pour in the freshly-squeezed, strained lemon juice. Stir in one can of Eagle Brand condensed milk with a wooden spoon. It will get sort of think and certainly creamy in consistency.

Carefully pour the lemon juice/milk mixture into the flat bowl, so the sweet stuff covers the vanilla wafer crumbs. Line all around the sides of the bowl with whole, round vanilla wafers.

Cover bowl and place in the refrigerator, until the mixture appears to have become more solid (less runny) in consistency. It's best to do this the day before—or at least several hours before—you plan to serve it. It will get quite solid.

When you are ready to serve it, cover the top of the whole thing with freshly-whipped whipping cream and serve with a spoon.

The whole thing can be doubled in size by using two cans of Eagle-Brand condensed milk and one-and-a-half cups of freshly squeezed lemon juice (plus more crushed vanilla wafers). Usually one small carton of whipping cream, or thick cream that you whip, is adequate for doubling the recipe.

Jack Daniels won a silver medal in the modern pentathlon at the 1956 Olympic Games and bronze medal at the 1960 Olympic Games. He has coached some of the best runners in the U.S., and is one of the most highly regarded distance running coaches in the world.

NOTES FROM THE CHEF: Here is a great recipe my mother, Louise, passed along. It makes a great after-dinner sweet or is even one of my favorites for breakfast or midday (with really cold skim milk).

Oatmeal Cookies w/ Raisins, Chocolate Chips, and Walnuts Jenelle Deatherage

I N G R E D I E N T S

1/2 c. Land-o-Lakes butter

1 c. firmly packed light brown sugar (C&H brand, with zip-top bag)

1 c. granulated sugar

2 eggs

1-1/2 tsp. real vanilla extract

3/4 c. unbleached white flour

3/4 c. whole wheat flour

1 tsp. baking soda

1/2 tsp. cinnamon

1/2 tsp. salt

3 c. quick oats

Raisins (Dole)

Chocolate chips (Ghirardelli dark)

Walnuts

Preheat oven to 350°. Soften butter, then beat together with both sugars, eggs, and vanilla until well-mixed and creamy.

In a separate bowl, combine the flours, baking soda, cinnamon, and salt. Combine with butter and sugar mixture, and mix well.

Stir in oats, raisins, chocolate chips, and walnuts. Drop rounded tablespoonfuls onto ungreased cookie sheet and bake for 12 minutes.

NOTES FROM THE CHEF:
I'm not really sure where this recipe came from. I've had it memorized for years. I think that it may be a modified version of the recipe on the back of the oatmeal canister. These cookies are one of my favorite things to bake in the cold Minneapolis winters, and they're reasonably healthy (as far as cookies go). My grandparents give me walnuts from the walnut trees on their farm, so this is also a nice way to put them to use!

Jenelle Deatherage finished second in the 1,500 at the 2008 USA Indoor Track & Field Championships, and represented the U.S. at the 2004 and 2008 World Indoor Championships. She finished fourth in the 1,500 at the 2004 U.S. Olympic Trials.

Chocolate Chip Pecan Pumpkin Cookies   Elva Dryer

I N G R E D I E N T S

1 c. all-purpose flour

1 c. whole wheat flour

1/4 c. rolled oats

1 tsp. baking powder

1 tsp. baking soda

1 tsp. ground cinnamon

1 tsp. ground nutmeg

1/2 tsp. salt

1/2 c. brown sugar

1/4 c. granulated sugar

1/2 c. butter, softened

1 c. pure pumpkin

1 large egg

1 tsp. vanilla extract

1/2 c. chopped pecans

1 c. semisweet chocolate chips

Preheat oven to 350°. Combine flour, oats, baking powder, baking soda, cinnamon, and nutmeg in bowl and set aside. Blend sugar and butter in large bowl. Beat egg and vanilla extract in small bowl, and then add to sugar and butter mixture along with pumpkin. Mix in flour mixture a cup at a time. Add chopped pecans and chocolate chips.

Place tablespoon sized or small ice cream scoop sized mounds on baking sheet. Bake for approximately 18-20 minutes. Cool on baking sheet for two to three minutes. Makes about 18 cookies.

> NOTES FROM THE CHEF: These cookies are more bread-like than chewy gooey. I came up with these as a way to use up some leftover pumpkin after Thanksgiving. They have turned into a favorite as a pre- or post-run snack.

Elva Dryer is a 2000 U.S. Olympian at 5,000m, and a 2004 U.S. Olympian at 10,000m.

Butterscotch and Chocolate Chip Cookies Suzy Favor Hamilton

I N G R E D I E N T S

2 sticks Parkay margarine

3/4 c. sugar

3/4 c. brown sugar

2 eggs

1 tsp. vanilla

1 tsp. salt

1 tsp. baking soda

1 c. butterscotch chips

2 c. chocolate chips

1/2 c. M&Ms (optional)

2-1/4 c. flour

Preheat oven to 350°. Mix the margarine and sugars, then add the eggs and vanilla. Mix well. In a separate bowl, mix the baking soda, salt, and flour. Gradually add the flour mixture to the margarine and sugar mixture, until consistency is uniform. Add all of the chips, stir with spoon.

Bake for approximately 11 minutes.

NOTES FROM THE CHEF: When I train hard, I crave sweets a lot. I would always keep chocolate chip cookie dough in my refrigerator so I could have fresh baked cookies at night after dinner. My husband shared in this special treat with me. For a healthier snack, my favorite is plain rice cakes dipped in chocolate!

Suzy Favor Hamilton is a three-time U.S. Olympian. She won nine NCAA titles for the University of Wisconsin and seven U.S. titles on the track. She ran under 4:00 in the 1,500m five times, with a best of 3:57.40.

Rolled Oat Cookies   Doris Heritage

I N G R E D I E N T S

1/2 c. oil

1 c. brown sugar

1 c. sugar

Less than 1 c. honey, with some molasses mixed in

1/3 c. milk (I used powdered milk)

1/2 c. raisins (I add a bit more, or dried cranberries, blueberries, or even fresh blueberries or chocolate chips)

1/2 c. (or more) nuts

1-1/2 c. flour

1/2 tsp. baking soda

1/4 tsp. baking powder

1 tsp. cinnamon, cloves, or nutmeg (I like ginger instead of nutmeg. If you use chocolate chips, go easy on the spices.)

1-1/2 c. oats

Preheat oven to 375°. Combine oil, both sugars, honey, and molasses. Sift together the powdered milk, flour, baking soda, baking powder, and the spice(s).

Mix flour mixture into sugar mixture. Add the oats and stir. Add the nuts and fruit/chocolate chips.

Spoon dough onto cookie sheet. Bake at 375° until cookies are done. Baking time depends on the size.

> NOTES FROM THE CHEF: This is my grandmother's recipe from Norway.

Doris Heritage was a 1968 and 1972 U.S. Olympian, with a best finish of fifth in the 800 in Mexico City. She won five consecutive World Cross Country titles from 1967 to 1971. Heritage won 14 national titles and set world records in the 440, 800, mile, and 3,000m.

Mexican Wedding Cakes   Jenny Crain

I N G R E D I E N T S

2 c. flour

1 c. shortening

4 tbsp. powdered sugar

1/2 c. nuts

2 tsp. vanilla

Preheat oven to 350°. Combine flour, shortening, vanilla, and nuts. Roll dough into small balls on greased cookie sheet. Bake until brown, then coat cookies with powdered sugar.

Jenny Crain holds PRs of 2:37:36 (marathon) and 32:30 (10,000 meters). She has represented the U.S. internationally, was the top U.S. finisher at the 2004 ING New York City Marathon, and is a four-time U.S. Olympic Marathon Trials qualifier.

I N G R E D I E N T S

1 c. all-purpose flour

3/4 c. packed light brown sugar

1/4 c. unsweetened cocoa powder

1 egg, 2 egg whites

5 tbsp. margarine, melted

1/4 c. milk

1 tsp. vanilla

2 tbsp. semisweet chocolate chips

2 tbsp. coarsely chopped walnuts

Preheat oven to 350°. Grease and flour an eight-inch square pan; set aside. Combine flour, brown sugar, and cocoa in a medium bowl. Blend together egg, egg white, margarine, milk, and vanilla in medium bowl. Add to flour mixture, mix well. Pour into baking pan; sprinkle with chocolate chips and walnuts.

Bake brownies until they spring back when lightly touched in the center, about 30 minutes. Cool completely on wire rack.

Stephanie Rothstein was an All-American distance runner for UC-Santa Barbara. She represented the U.S. at the 2007 International Chiba Ekiden.

Perfect Chocolate Cake   Patti Dillon

I N G R E D I E N T S

2 c. sugar

1-3/4 c. all-purpose flour

3/4 c. cocoa (we use Hershey's)

1-1/2 tsp. baking powder

1-1/2 tsp. baking soda

1 tsp. salt

2 eggs

1 c. milk

1/2 c. vegetable oil

2 tsp. vanilla extract

1 c. boiling water

To make the cake, preheat oven to 350°. Grease and flour pan. (We use two nine-inch round baking pans.) Combine all dry ingredients in a large bowl. Stir. Add eggs, milk, oil, and vanilla. Beat on medium speed for two minutes. Stir in boiling water; batter will be thin.

NOTES FROM THE CHEF:
My son, Aaron Dillon, makes this cake, and my daughter, Raven Dillon, makes the frosting. Both are Connecticut Junior Olympians. We enjoy dessert. There's nothing like a homemade chocolate cake to top off a good dinner. (It's a good thing we run!)

Pour batter into two pans. Bake for about 30 to 35 minutes, or until toothpick comes out clean. Cool on rack. After cooling about 10 minutes, remove cake from pans. Cool completely before frosting.

I N G R E D I E N T S

2-1/2 sticks unsalted butter, softened

1 c. confectioners' sugar

3/4 c. Dutch-processed cocoa

Pinch of table salt

3/4 c. of light corn syrup

1 tsp. vanilla extract

8 oz. chocolate (more if you eat it while you're making it), melted and cooled a little*

*The frosting may be made with milk, semisweet or bittersweet chocolate. We enjoy using milk chocolate.

Put the butter, sugar, cocoa, and salt in a food processor and mix until smooth (about 30 seconds).

Add the corn syrup and vanilla, and mix just until they are combined (about 10 seconds). Add the chocolate and pulse until smooth and creamy (about 15 seconds). Frost cake and enjoy!

This frosting recipe is adapted from a recipe which appeared in the March/April 2008 issue of *Cook's Illustrated* magazine.

Patti Dillon was the first American woman to break 2:30 in the marathon. She once held world bests for 5 miles, 10k, 20k, the half marathon, and 30k. She has been inducted into the National Distance Running Hall of Fame.

Chocolate Chip Carrot Cake w/ Cream Cheese Frosting Amy Yoder Begley

I N G R E D I E N T S

1-1/2 c. unsifted all-purpose flour

3/4 c. sugar

1/2 c. packed light brown sugar

1-1/4 tsp. baking soda

1-1/2 tsp. vanilla

2 c. (12 oz. package) semisweet chocolate mini chips

1 tsp. cinnamon

1/2 tsp. salt

3 eggs

3/4 c. vegetable oil

2 c. grated carrots

1/2 c. chopped walnuts (optional)

To make the cake, preheat oven to 350°. In a large bowl, combine the flour, sugars, baking soda, salt, and cinnamon and stir until uniformly mixed. In a small bowl, beat together the eggs, oil, and vanilla. Add egg mixture to dry mixture and mix well.

Stir in the carrots, chocolate chips, and walnuts. Grease and flour a 13x9-inch pan and pour in mixture. Bake for 35 to 40 minutes, or until an inserted toothpick comes out clean. Let cake cool completely before frosting.

> NOTES FROM THE CHEF: I don't use the walnuts. Regular chocolate chips work just fine. I substitute applesauce for all, or at least half of, the vegetable oil. To make it gluten free, I use Bob's Red Mill All-Purpose Baking Flour. I also flour the pan with a mix of flour and baking cocoa powder. This is my favorite cake recipe; I make it when I want to indulge. I figure the equal parts of carrot and chocolate chips make it halfway healthy. But the frosting is great too.

I N G R E D I E N T S

1 3 oz. package cream cheese, softened

1/4 c. butter or margarine, softened

2 c. powdered sugar

1 tsp. vanilla

To make the frosting, beat the cream cheese and butter together in a small mixing bowl until smooth and uniformly mixed. Add the powdered sugar gradually. Mix in the vanilla and continue beating until mixture is smooth. Frost cake once it has cooled.

These are adapted from recipes which originally appeared in the *Hershey's Chocolate Treasury* cookbook.

Amy Yoder Begley was a two-time NCAA champion and 15-time All-American for the University of Arkansas. She won the 2004 USA 10k title and the 2007 Manchester Road Race.

INGREDIENTS

5 oz. graham crackers (about 9 crackers), broken in pieces
2 tbsp. sugar
5 tbsp. unsalted melted butter

To make the crust, preheat oven to 325°. In a food processor, pulse crackers and sugar until they are finely grounded (about 15 seconds). Add the melted butter through the feed tube, until the mixture resembles wet sand. Transfer mixture to a pie plate and spread evenly on bottom and sides. Bake for approximately 15 minutes and cool on a rack.

INGREDIENTS

3 tbsp. of cold orange juice
2 tsp. vanilla extract
2 tsp. gelatin
1 c. cold heavy cream
2/3 c. sugar
3/4 tsp. table salt
1 tsp. cinnamon
1/2 tsp. ginger
1/4 tsp. nutmeg
1/8 tsp. ground cloves
3 large egg yolks
1 15 oz. can (1-3/4 c.) plain pumpkin puree

To make the filling, stir the orange juice and vanilla together in a bowl. Sprinkle gelatin over the mixture and set aside to thicken (about five minutes).

In a small saucepan, combine one-half cup of the heavy cream, one-third cup of the sugar, and all of the salt and spices. Cook over medium-low heat until bubbles form at the edges, then remove from heat.

In a medium bowl, whisk together the remaining one-third cup of sugar and the egg yolks until the mixture is pale and has thickened slightly. Slowly pour in the hot cream mixture, whisking constantly.

Return the mixture to the saucepan and cook over medium-low heat, stirring constantly and making sure to scrape the bottom of the pan. Do this until the custard has thickened (approximately two minutes).

Immediately pour the custard over the gelatin mixture, and stir until it's smooth and the gelatin has completely dissolved.

In a food processor, purée the pumpkin until it is smooth. With the food processor running, add the remaining one-half cup of the heavy cream through the feed tube in a steady stream (about 15 seconds).

Combine pumpkin and cream mixture with gelatin/custard mixture and mix well. Transfer filling to cooled crust. Chill pie, uncovered, until filling is just set (about three hours). Cover pie with plastic wrap and chill for an additional six hours.

Cut pie and serve.

NOTES FROM THE CHEF: You can either purchase a graham cracker crust or make your own. We make our own, because it's always better.

Patti Dillon was the first American woman to break 2:30 in the marathon. She once held world bests for 5 miles, 10k, 20k, the half marathon, and 30k. She has been inducted into the National Distance Running Hall of Fame.

Swedish Apple Pie   Sara and Ryan Hall

I N G R E D I E N T S

4 c. sliced, peeled apples
2 tbsp. brown sugar
1 tsp. cinnamon
1/2 c. butter (must be butter!)
Pinch of salt
1 c. sugar
1 c. flour
1 egg
1/2 c. chopped nuts

Preheat oven to 350°. Fill a nine-inch pie plate with the sliced, peeled apples. Sprinkle with brown sugar and cinnamon.

Mix the butter, salt, sugar, flour, egg, and nuts together; spread on top of apples. Bake for one hour and serve warm with vanilla ice cream.

This pie "makes its own crust."

Sara (Bei) Hall is the 2006 USA 5k champion. Hall was a seven-time All-American and three-time NCAA runner-up for Stanford University. She finished third at the 2003 NCAA Cross Country Championships and led Stanford to the team title.

Ryan Hall is a 2008 U.S. Olympian in the marathon, by virtue of his dominant win at the 2008 U.S. Olympic Marathon Trials. He holds the U.S. half marathon record of 59:43, and has run 2:06:17 in the marathon.

NOTES FROM THE CHEF: This comes from my mother, Karen Bei. It's a Bei family recipe that is very special to us, because Ryan and I served this pie instead of wedding cake at our wedding! We actually made 40 pies, along with some of my family and mom's friends, the week of the wedding! I have never met anyone that doesn't like it, and it is much easier to make than normal apple pies! —Sara Hall

Amy's Apple Crisp
Amy Rudolph

I N G R E D I E N T S

8-10 apples
1/2 c. sugar
3 c. Bisquick or Jiffy mix
1 c. sugar
1 tsp. cinnamon (plus a sprinkle)
2 eggs, beaten
1/2 c. shortening or butter, melted

Preheat oven to 400°. Grease the bottom of a 9x13-inch glass or metal pan. Peel and core the apples. Slice apples into pan (just leave some room for the topping). Sprinkle with loose cinnamon and one-half cup of sugar.

In a bowl, combine the Bisquick, sugar, and a teaspoon of cinnamon. Slowly pour in the egg and mix with a fork until crumbly. Sprinkle mixture over apples.

Pour melted shortening or butter over apples and topping. Bake for 25 to 30 minutes, or until golden brown.

NOTES FROM THE CHEF: This recipe can be cut in half; just use an 8x8-inch pan. My mom always made this for me growing up, and it has become one of my specialties in the kitchen. You can substitute pears for the apples and in the summer you can use frozen fruit (strawberries, peaches, mixed berries). It tastes best when served warm with vanilla ice cream. Enjoy!

Amy Rudolph is a 1996 and 2000 U.S. Olympian at 5,000m. She has won national titles on the roads, indoor track, outdoor track, and in cross country.

Nutty Chocolate Chip Ice Cream Sandwiches   Shannon Rowbury

I N G R E D I E N T S

1 tsp. vanilla

1/2 c. butter at room temperature

1/2 c. brown sugar

1/2 c. white granulated sugar

1 large egg

1 c. all-purpose flour, sifted

1/2 tsp. baking soda

1/2 tsp. baking powder

1/2 tsp. salt

1 c. (6 oz.) chocolate chips

2 c. chopped walnuts

1/2 c. shredded dry coconut (preferably unsweetened)

Ice cream or frozen yogurt (vanilla is good)

Shannon Rowbury won the 2007 NCAA Indoor mile title for Duke University. One year later, running professionally for Nike, she won the 2008 USA Indoor 3,000m title.

Cream together the vanilla, butter, white sugar, brown sugar, and egg until well-blended and smooth in consistency. In a separate bowl, mix the flour, baking soda, baking powder, and salt together; add to the egg/sugar mixture and blend well. Add the chocolate chips, walnuts, and coconut, and blend well.

Use a small ice cream scoop to make uniformly-sized cookie balls. You can bake whatever you want to eat now, and freeze the remaining cookie balls for later.

To bake cookies, preheat oven to 350°. Put cookie balls onto ungreased cookie tray. To make dense, chewy cookies, bake for approximately five minutes, then take cookie tray out of the oven and drop it on a hard surface. This will cause the cookies to "collapse" as they are cooking, which makes them more chewy. Continue this process every five minutes, until the cookies are browned and the middle of the cookie looks ready (it shouldn't look raw in the middle). The cookies normally take about 15 minutes to bake in our oven.

To assemble the ice cream sandwiches, first let the cookies cool completely. Place one small scoop of ice cream on top of one cookie. Place a second cookie on top of the ice cream, and gently press together until the ice cream is evenly distributed between the two cookies. Wrap in plastic wrap or wax paper, and place in freezer for a few hours, until ice cream hardens.

NOTES FROM THE CHEF: My aunt, Karen Sue Hovde, created this recipe several years ago. She died of ovarian cancer in November of 2001, but her cookies are still one of my favorite desserts. You can eat them with a tall glass of milk, or make them into ice cream sandwiches, which we do every Thanksgiving in memory of Sue.

Mint Oreo Ice Cream Cake

Sara and Steve Slattery

I N G R E D I E N T S

4 c. Oreo cookie crumbs (or plain chocolate cookie crumbs)

1/2 c. melted butter or shortening

1/2 gallon cookies and cream ice cream (a quality ice cream)

3 c. Cool Whip

1-1/2 c. marshmallow cream

2 tsp. mint extract

Chocolate sauce

Combine the cookie crumbs and butter. Press into the bottom of a large Pyrex dish. Freeze for 30 minutes.

Thaw Oreo ice cream until soft but not runny. Spread on top of oreo cookie crust. Freeze for 30 to 60 minutes.

Thaw Cool Whip until soft. Microwave marshmallow cream in microwave for 30 seconds, and mix with Cool Whip and mint extract until smooth. Spread on top of ice cream evenly. Freeze for 60 minutes.

Before serving, sprinkle some leftover cookie crumbs on top of cake and top with a swirl of chocolate sauce.

> NOTES FROM THE CHEF: This is one of our favorite recipes. Steve and I aren't big cake eaters. And, as a kid growing up my grandmother would always make me grasshopper mint pie for my birthday instead of cake, and Steve would always have Carvel ice cream cake. So, when we started dating, for Steve's birthday, I decided I would combine the two and make mint ice cream cake.
> —*Sara Slattery*

Sara Slattery was a two-time NCAA champion for the University of Colorado. As a professional runner, she finished second in the 10,000m at the 2006 USA Outdoor Track & Field Championships and won the 2006 Bolder Boulder 10k.

Steve Slattery is the 2003 USA champion in the 3,000m steeplechase. He represented the U.S. in the steeplechase at the 2003 and 2005 World Track & Field Championships.

Banana "Ice Cream" (or Shake)   Amy Yoder Begley

I N G R E D I E N T S

Ripe Bananas

Liquid of choice: milk, soy milk, chocolate milk, etc.

Add-ins of choice: fruit, peanut butter, chocolate sauce, chocolate chips, etc.

Peel and cut ripe bananas in half or thirds. Place ripe bananas in a plastic bag and put in the freezer. Once they are frozen, take out the desired amount of banana.

Put the bananas and your choice of liquid and add-ins in a blender. Blend until it has reached the desired consistency. Use less liquid to make ice cream, or more liquid to make a shake.

NOTES FROM THE CHEF:
My favorite combination is bananas and chocolate soy milk. If I want a real treat, I add peanut butter and dark chocolate pieces to it.

This is adapted from a recipe which was originally published by the Pritikin Longevity Center.

Amy Yoder Begley was a two-time NCAA champion and 15-time All-American for the University of Arkansas. She won the 2004 USA 10k title and the 2007 Manchester Road Race.

Sticky Date Pudding with Butterscotch Sauce   Craig Mottram

I N G R E D I E N T S

1-3/4 c. packed pitted dates

1 c. orange juice

1 c. water

3 eggs

6 tbsp. unsalted butter

2 c. all-purpose flour

1/2 tsp. salt

1 c. granulated sugar

1/2 tsp. ground ginger

1/4 tsp. nutmeg

1-1/2 tsp. baking soda

1/2 tsp. baking powder

A pinch of love

To make the pudding, preheat oven to 350°. In a medium-sized saucepan, simmer the chopped dates in water and orange juice. After five minutes, remove the saucepan from heat and stir in baking soda. Let stand for 15 minutes.

Then, place butter and sugar in a large bowl, and blend ingredients until mixture has a fluffy texture. Add eggs, flour, baking powder, salt, ginger, and nutmeg. Once again, mix until well combined.

Pour batter into lightly greased pudding or muffin tray (preferably silicone) and bake for one hour.

Once baked, let pudding cool slightly for 10 minutes.

> NOTES FROM THE CHEF: Sticky date pudding is a favorite Australian dessert, great for celebrating a win with family and friends, guaranteed to make the taste of success even sweeter! This recipe was submitted by Mottram's partner, Krystine Horfiniak.

Craig Mottram is an Australian Olympian and record holder, who has run 12:55.76 for 5,000m. He won a bronze medal in the 5,000m at the 2005 World Track & Field Championships and a silver medal in the 5,000m at the 2006 Commonwealth Games.

I N G R E D I E N T S

1-1/2 c. brown sugar

200 g. (just under 1 c.) unsalted butter

1 c. cream

1/2 tsp. vanilla

To make the butterscotch sauce, combine the brown sugar, butter, cream, and vanilla in a saucepan and stir mixture over low heat, until sauce thickens.

Serve pudding warm, drizzled in butterscotch sauce, with a side of vanilla ice cream.

Oma's Lemon Slice
Victoria Mitchell

INGREDIENTS

2 packets Marie biscuits, crushed

1 can sweetened condensed milk

250 g. butter (one heaping cup), melted

2 c. coconut

Rind off one lemon

Crush biscuits in plastic bag with rolling pin. Combine coconut and rind with crushed biscuits. Add melted butter and condensed milk to dry ingredients. Stir. Place mixture in glass tray and press down. Put in fridge and allow to set.

INGREDIENTS

Confectioners' sugar

Juice of a lemon

Additional coconut

To make the icing, use confectioners' sugar and the lemon juice (no water) to make a thick-ish icing. Ice slice and sprinkle with coconut.

NOTES FROM THE CHEF: This is my favorite lemon slice recipe, which my grandma used to use. It's simple yet sooo tasty!

Victoria Mitchell is an Australian steeplechase champion, and she also won the 2005 NCAA steeplechase title for Butler University. She has run 9:30.84 for the 3,000m steeplechase, and has represented Australia at the Commonwealth Games and World Championships.

Rainbow Jello

INGREDIENTS

- 1 packet of red jello
- 1 packet of orange jello
- 1 packet of yellow jello
- 1 packet of green jello
- 6 tbsp. gelatin
- 1 can of condensed milk

To make the colored layer, stir one tablespoon of gelatin into the red jello crystals, then add one cup of boiling water. Pour into lasagna dish or similar and set.

To make a white layer, pour two tablespoons of gelatin into cold water to soften. Stir one cup of boiling water into condensed milk, then add gelatin mixture and stir until smooth. When cool, pour one-third of the white mixture onto the set red jello. Place dish back in the refrigerator to set.

Repeat above steps using orange, yellow and green jello, alternating colored layers with white layers.

Cut into squares and present in a glass dish. Looks impressive!

NOTES FROM THE CHEF: This was given to me by my mum, Katrina Jenkins. I love making this jelly (jello) to take to a barbecue. It's a fun dessert that always impresses guests. It is low in fat (high in sugar!) and is also great just to have in the fridge for a quick snack.

Sarah Jamieson is an Australian Olympian and record holder. She won a silver medal in the 1,500m at the 2006 Commonwealth Games.

Strawberry Jello Parfait   Christin Wurth-Thomas

I N G R E D I E N T S

2 boxes strawberry jello

1 pint of sliced strawberries

Vanilla ice cream

Prepare one box of strawberry jello according to directions on box. Before putting jello in refrigerator to cool, add the pint of sliced strawberries, then let it set as usual.

To make the topping, bring the second box of jello to a boil as directed on the box. Remove from heat and let it cool for 15 to 20 minutes. *Do not* add water after you have brought the jello to a boil.

Beat one to two cups of ice cream into the latter batch of jello, until mixture is creamy (roughly one to two minutes). After base of jello has set (two to three hours), add ice cream topping. Serves four to five people.

NOTES FROM THE CHEF: This is my favorite jello salad or dessert, which my mom always makes around the holidays.

Christin Wurth-Thomas was an All-American runner for the University of Arkansas. She finished second in the 1,500m at the 2007 USA Outdoor Track & Field Championships and second in the mile at the 2007 USA Indoor Track & Field Championships. She has represented the U.S. at the World Cross Country Championships and World Track & Field Championships.

Note From the Editor:

As someone who relies almost solely on a microwave for all of her cooking, I never imagined myself compiling, editing, and laying out a cookbook. However, I never imagined that two of the events that shook the distance running community in 2007—the sudden death of Ryan Shay during the U.S. Olympic Marathon Trials, and Jenny Crain being hit by a car while out on a training run and suffering a serious brain injury—would happen either. All of the proceeds of this cookbook are being donated to the Ryan Shay Memorial Fund and the Jenny Crain "Make It Happen" Fund.

This cookbook is not a traditional one in many senses, and it might be a little rougher around the edges than the other ones you have sitting on your shelves at home, but it is an example of our great distance running community coming together. I contacted as many athletes as I could reach, explaining the project and asking, "What's your favorite recipe?" The athletes responded with great enthusiasm, and the recipes and comments they sent far surpassed my expectations.

I can't promise that making or eating any of the foods in the preceding pages will make you a world-class distance runner, but I can assure that these are recipes that have been tested and enjoyed by some of the world's best distance runners.

Thank you for your support of this project.

Alison Wade
May, 2008

Special Thanks:

In addition to all of the athletes who contributed recipes, I would like to thank the following individuals for their invaluable contributions to this project:

Parker Morse, Becky Wexler, Peter Gambaccini, Donna Crain, Alicia Shay, Barbara Huebner, Chris Layne, Lisa Buster, Chris Marcel, Kimberly Holland, Cheryl Neumann, Gavin Pavey, Marla Runyan, Stephanie McCray, Krystine Horfiniak, Kalin Ritzenhein, Matt Taylor, Sam Grotewold, Brad Hudson, Toby Warden, Pat Goodwin, Dave Milner, Scott Douglas, Shauneen Garrahan, Heather Wilson, Caitlin Klinedinst, Ricky Simms, Ricky Quintana, the Shutesbury Coffee Cake Runners, New York Road Runners, and Ruth, George, Courtney, Jennifer, Beth, and Izzy Wade.

Breinigsville, PA USA
14 October 2009

225806BV00003B/49/P

9 781435 716407